RIVER
FLY-FISHING

RIVER FLY-FISHING

The Complete Guide

PETER LAPSLEY

Illustrated by Calum Mackintosh

ROBERT HALE · LONDON

© *Peter Lapsley 2003*
First published in Great Britain 2003

ISBN 978 0 7090 7122 8

Robert Hale Limited
Clerkenwell House
Clerkenwell Green
London EC1R 0HT

www.halebooks.com

A catalogue record for this book is available from the British Library

4 6 8 10 9 7 5

Typeset in 10/14 Palatino
Derek Doyle & Associates, Shaw Heath.
Printed and bound in Great Britain by
Biddles Limited, King's Lynn

Contents

Acknowledgements

Much of what I know about river fly-fishing has been learnt from the many friends with whom I have been fortunate enough to fish over the years. To try to list them risks omitting some and thus, perhaps, causing offence. But I am especially grateful to Fred Buller, David Beazley, Ron Clark, Brian Clarke, Mike Davis, Donald Downs, John Fairrie, Warren Gilchrist, John Goddard, Nick Gooderham, Ron Holloway, Charles Jardine, the late Robin Lee, Professor Norman Maclean, Robin and Nicky Mulholland, Dr Conor Nolan, Neil Patterson, David Profumo, Bill Rathbone, Iain Shield, Paddy Vincent, Simon Ward, Eric Williams and Barney Wilson – all wonderful waterside companions, great fun to fish with and most generous in sharing their knowledge and expertise.

Similarly generous away from the waterside have been my friends Dr Cyril Bennett, Peter Hayes, Nick Lyons, Charles Rangely-Wilson and Mike Weaver.

Deserving of special thanks, and in a class of their own, are Roy Darlington and Stewart Newell who manage the magical and historic Abbotts Barton fishery on the River Itchen, which I have been fortunate to be able to fish for getting on for twenty years. Their commitment to this remarkable water is legendary, and I enjoy my time there as much for their company as for the fishing itself.

I am most grateful, also, to Charles Inniss at the Half Moon Inn at Sheepwash, Richard Slocock, the proprietor of Wessex Fly Fishing, and Anne Voss Bark and her instructors at The Arundell Arms, Roy Buckingham and David Pilkington, for all the kindness and help they offered when we were taking the photographs for the book.

Warm thanks are due, too, to Barry Unwin and his staff at Fulling Mill Flies, producers of flies of quite exceptional quality, who provided all the patterns shown in the colour plates; to Terry Griffiths for having taken such outstanding photographs of them; to Mark Bowler, editor of *Fly Fishing & Fly Tying*, for his photographs of that splendid Spey trout and of the River Lyon, to Calum Mackintosh for the excellent drawings with which the text is illustrated; and to Martin Kendall and Susan Hale, at Robert Hale for their patience with me and their enthusiasm for the book.

Finally, particular thanks are due to my beloved wife, Liza, who is so extraordinarily tolerant of the time I take both to fish and to write, so selflessly supportive of me in everything I do, and who took the vast majority of the photographs for the book.

Foreword

As I looked out of my window at the magical little River Lyd, on a cold, bright February morning, I was overwhelmed by the beauty of the stream and the thought of a new trout-fishing season about to start.

This latest book by Peter Lapsley captures so perfectly the charm and the challenge of river fly-fishing for trout, sea trout and grayling. It is a book that will appeal equally to the experienced angler and to the newcomer. It covers every aspect of the sport, from its history, the rivers we fish, the characteristics of the fish, their habits and food, to the tackle and techniques used to catch them.

I particularly welcome Peter's emphasis on the fact that river trout fly-fishing is by no means an exclusive or costly pursuit. The useful section entitled 'Signposts' guides would-be flyfishers to affordable and readily accessible rivers throughout Britain.

I was interested in his thesis that not only are brown trout and sea trout the same species, now accepted as fact by scientists, but that all brown trout have a migratory instinct and are therefore potentially sea trout; this is greatly encouraging for future sea-trout runs.

Peter's 'new' treatment of the life cycle of the up-winged fly will be of interest to the more experienced fly fisherman and, where artificial flies are concerned, he wisely avoids promoting the more esoteric patterns, which can be so confusing for the novice angler.

His chapter on the future of the sport is both important and sobering, listing as it does the alarming decline in fly life on the chalk streams, the collapse of sea-trout stocks due to estuarine salmon farming and predation by fish-eating birds.

All in all, this is a wonderfully comprehensive book by a writer and fisherman who possesses that rare ability to explain complicated subjects simply. I commend it highly to all those interested in fly-fishing on rivers for trout, sea trout and grayling – 'old hands' or newcomers to the sport.

Anne Voss Bark
Lifton, Devon

Illustrations

Between pages 64 and 65

Colour photographs

Between pages 160 and 161

Between pages 112 and 113

Black and white photographs

Line drawings

Illustration Credits

Mark Bowler: 2 & 21. R.B. Broughton: 26. Terry Griffiths – flies supplied by Fulling Mill Ltd: 27 & 28. Simon Brown: 29. Calum Mackintosh: Figs 1–23.

Introduction

Those of us who fish for trout, sea trout and grayling in Britain should count ourselves extremely fortunate to have such a wealth of water available to us. Although waiting lists for clubs and syndicates on the chalk streams of southern and eastern England can be quite long and membership of them can be expensive, there is a mass of wonderful streams and rivers in Dorset and the West Country, in the north of England and in Ireland, Scotland and Wales offering marvellous sport and ready access at very modest cost.

In truth, many of these accessible waters are more attractive and interesting to fish than 'exclusive' chalk-stream fisheries. Such is the demand for chalk-stream fishing in populous south-east England that rod-pressure tends to be high. Wild fish populations are often insufficiently robust to meet such heavy demand and have to be augmented or even replaced with (frequently unnaturally large) farm-reared stock fish. With carefully managed banks and weed beds, and more or less smart car parks and fishing huts, such fisheries can have an artificiality about them that, while pleasantly pampering, is far removed from the stalking of wild fish in more natural waters.

The chief purpose of this book, therefore, is to encourage flyfishers and would-be flyfishers to explore some of the wonderful river fly-fishing these islands offer, and to help them enjoy it to the full. As a part of that, it seeks also to promote the grayling as the splendid game fish it is, and to de-bunk the myth that there are no longer any sea-trout runs in our rivers. It is certainly true that estuarine salmon farming has done catastrophic damage to sea-trout runs in some rivers, especially in

Scotland. Elsewhere, though, sea trout continue to thrive and to offer spectacularly exciting and productive fishing.

One of the great attractions of fly-fishing is that each of us can take what we want from it, and that what we want may change over time. Certainly, having been immersed in the sport for almost fifty years, I have gone through several stages. For a while, every fish I caught, large or small, was a trophy. Then there was a period during which, having become passably competent, I sought to catch large numbers of fish. For a long time, I was interested only in catching fish on flies I had tied myself. Then, having been reminded by the late Dick Walker of his adage that if you can catch one fish you can catch lots of fish, I became chiefly interested in catching big fish. Eventually, I became intrigued by difficult fish, particularly fussy feeders or fish in especially difficult lies. Nowadays, and while I still enjoy my fishing hugely, I find I get at least as much enjoyment from being in nice places with nice people, from watching others fish and from the wildlife of the waterside as I do from the fishing itself.

Personally, I have derived a very great deal of pleasure from exploring some of the sport's more obscure corners and crevices – fish behaviour, entomology, fly-tying, tackle development, casting techniques and angling history among them. Such preoccupation with the detail of the sport is by no means necessary. I shall always remember my late father, who came to fishing in middle age, listening patiently as I explained some esoteric entomological phenomenon to him and then saying quietly, 'You know, I don't really want to be very good at this; I just want to enjoy it.' The lesson was well learnt.

Therefore, in writing this book, I have sought to strike a practical balance between those two extremes – between determined dufferhood on the one hand and unnecessary esotericism on the other. I have sought also to un-pick some of the mystique that has been built up around river fly-fishing, especially where natural flies are concerned. I am wary of those who claim to be able to tell the difference between a medium olive and a small spurwing at twenty paces, or who use Latin names to describe flies. Only very rarely do trout and grayling show a marked preference for one species of natural fly over another of comparable size and hue, and they certainly do not understand Latin.

So I have not included the distinguishing features of the several dozen natural flies that are of interest to fish and thus to fishermen, nor have I littered the text with their taxonomic names.

Some people who have written books on fly-fishing have used them as vehicles to promote the artificial fly patterns they have designed, which can only be copied by those who are themselves fly dressers. It seems to me to be quite wrong to suppose that everyone who goes fishing ties his or her own flies or wants to do so. So, all of the flies mentioned in the text or illustrated in the colour plates are available for purchase from tackle shops or through mail order catalogues.

Finally, it would be wrong to forget the not inconsiderable problems fly-fishing is facing. We owe it to ourselves, our fellow anglers and future generations of anglers to do whatever we can to increase public respect for our sport and to assure its future. I am aware that the chapter on that subject, 'Looking Ahead', makes rather gloomy reading, but make no apology for that. We must face up to the difficulties facing angling and address them actively. If we do not, there is a real risk that the sport will wither away, and that would be a tragedy.

1   Roots

Fly-fishing is a remarkably ancient pursuit with a recorded history stretching back almost two thousand years, albeit with one huge gap. An understanding of the ways in which it has evolved provides a fascinating and colourful backdrop to our sport and is important to understanding why we fish as we do today.

Claudius Aelianus, usually referred to as Ælian, lived from about AD 170 to AD 235. A Roman scholar who wrote chiefly in Greek, he rarely left Rome, much of his material being obtained from earlier writers and from hearsay. That does nothing to diminish his importance to angling literature. In the first chapter of Book XV of his seventeen-volume magnum opus, *De Natura Animalium* ('On the Nature of Animals'), a wonderful ramble through the animal kingdom, real and legendary, he provided us with the first known description of fly-fishing for trout, and extraordinarily vivid it is:

I have heard of a Macedonian way of catching fish, and it is this: between Borœa and Thessalonica runs a river called the Astræus, and in it there are fish with speckled skins; what the natives of the country call them you had better ask the Macedonians. These fish feed upon a fly peculiar to the country, which hovers on the river. It is not like the flies found elsewhere, nor does it resemble a wasp in appearance, nor in shape would one justly describe it as a midge or a bee, yet it has something of each of these. In boldness it is like a fly, in size you might call it a midge, it imitates the colour of a wasp, and it hums like a bee. The natives generally call it the Hippouros.

These flies seek their food over the river, but do not escape the observation of the fish swimming below. When then the fish observes a fly on the surface, it swims quietly up, afraid to stir the water above, lest it should scare away its prey; then coming up by its shadow, it opens its mouth gently and gulps down the fly, like a wolf carrying off a sheep from the fold or an eagle a goose from the farmyard; having done this it goes below the rippling water.

Now though the fishermen know this, they do not use these flies at all for bait for fish; for if a man's hand touch them, they lose their natural colour, their wings wither, and they become unfit food for the fish. For this reason they have nothing to do with them, hating them for their bad character; but they have planned a snare for the fish, and get the better of them by their fisherman's craft.

They fasten red (crimson red) wool around a hook, and fix on to the wool two feathers which grow under a cock's wattles, and which in colour are like wax. Their rod is six feet long, and their line is the same length. Then they throw their snare, and the fish, attracted and maddened by the colour, comes straight at it, thinking from the pretty sight to gain a dainty mouthful; when, however, it opens its jaws, it is caught by the hook, and enjoys a bitter repast, a captive.

This remarkable account is as intriguing for the conundrums it poses as for its descriptive brilliance. Where is the Astræus? Probably now incorporated into the Moglenítsas Regional Canal which runs into the River Aliákmon in northern Greece, and thence into the Ægean Sea. What species were the 'fish with speckled skins'? Almost certainly trout. What kind of fly was the Hippouros? Possibly a horsefly or a drone fly. And what did the Macedonian fisherman's fly look like? Impossible to say; there have probably been more attempted interpretations of this pattern than of any other.

Although there seem to have been no further written references to fly-fishing for almost a thousand years, it is inconceivable that it should have died out and then been reinvented in the fourteenth century. The absence of evidence for its continuation between the third and thirteenth centuries almost certainly has as much to do with its being taken for granted as a routine means of gathering food as with general illiteracy and a paucity of written material on any subject during the period.

With the growth of literature and literacy during the thirteenth and fourteenth centuries came tantalizing allusions to flies and fly-fishing. Rather than providing detailed descriptions of the pursuit, they showed it to be something most people were familiar with and that, certainly by the fourteenth century and probably much earlier, fly-fishing had become well developed and was being practised widely right across Europe, in Austria, Britain, Germany, Italy, Switzerland and Spain.

It was the arrival of printing in England that gave the world its first instructional book on fly-fishing. Westminster, where William Caxton had installed the first English press in 1474, was the centre for early British printing, and it was in the grounds of Westminster Abbey, twenty-two years later, in 1496, that Dame Juliana Berners' *The Treatise of Fishing with an Angle* was published by Wynkyn de Worde.

The *Treatise* was an appendix to the Dame's *Book of St Albans*, a manual on hawking, hunting and heraldry, and this of itself provides an interesting clue as to one of the ways in which attitudes to fly-fishing had changed over time. It seems reasonably clear from his account that Ælian's Macedonians used fly-fishing simply as a practical means of catching trout for the pot, rather than for sport. By Dame Juliana's day, angling had become a recreation. The *Treatise* represented angling as being comparable with other field sports – hunting, hawking and fowling – and set out rules on how it should be conducted, with rod, line and hook.

There has been much debate about who Dame Juliana was, whether she really wrote the book and when it was actually written. While intriguing to students of angling literature, such questions are largely academic. What is of greatest importance about the *Treatise* is that it provides us with the first detailed and authoritative account of the tackle and tactics used for angling.

The tackle of the times, quite comprehensively described by Dame

Juliana, was homespun and must have required as much skill in its manufacture as in its use. Rods, from 13 to 14 feet long, were of three pieces, with butts of blackthorn or medlar, middle sections of willow, hazel or ash, and tips of hazel. The upper ends of the butt and middle sections were made hollow with a red-hot spike to form female ferrules into which the next pieces were fitted.

The angler made his own hooks from square-headed needles, shaping them, cutting the barbs, flattening the ends and re-tempering them before whipping them to spun, tapered, knotted horsehair lines, anything from two to six strands thick at the point, marginally longer than the rods and attached to loops at the rod tips.

The Dame described the dressings for a dozen artificial flies, using wool of various colours for the bodies, and partridge, drake and buzzard feathers, and red cock hackles, as wings. Her flies do not appear to have been dressed with collar, beard or palmered hackles (hackles wound down the length of the shank) as ours tend to be, and the woollen bodies would quickly have become waterlogged, but she clearly understood at least the principles of dry-fly fishing, advocating the use of artificial flies fished on the surface when fish were rising. She was, however, no fly-fishing purist. An avowedly pragmatic angler, Dame Juliana was as content to fish for trout with caterpillars, worms, dapped natural flies or minnows as with dressed fly patterns, and to fish for pike, perch, roach, bream and dace as happily as for trout. This was to be a guiding philosophy for most anglers for the next 350 years.

In continental Europe, another and infinitely more tantalizing work – nowadays known as the Tegernsee manuscript – emanating from Bavaria, dates back to the same period as the *Treatise*. In script, rather than printed, it consists of thirteen leaves bound into untitled book form. Seemingly written by a scribe at Tegernsee Abbey as a means of gathering together local knowledge about catching fish, along with information plagiarized from a German booklet on the subject, the text is dogged by its author's own ignorance and apparent confusion. It is a strange mishmash of snippets of information about artificial flies (it catalogues some fifty for a wide variety of freshwater fish species), line making and fishing techniques, mixed in with advice on baits, on poisoning rivers and on tickling fish. What it does show, however, is the degree of sophistication central European angling had attained by the early fifteenth century.

The advanced state of development of Spanish fly-fishing at this time and the extent to which it had grown entirely separately from fly-fishing elsewhere is demonstrated by two fascinating books – Fernando Basurto's *Little Treatise on Fishing*, published in 1539, and Juan de Bergara's *El Manuscrito de Astorga*, written eighty-five years later, in 1624. Between them, they provide us with a remarkably clear and comprehensive picture of the fly-fishing tackle, techniques and tactics used in Spain in the sixteenth and seventeenth centuries and, in particular, of the advanced nature of Spanish trout-fly design – emphasizing the merits of tying flies specifically to represent the naturals on the water and describing complex patterns tied on spade-end hooks with silk bodies and multiple hackles in a rich variety of colours.

Back in England, the publication in 1651 of Thomas Barker's *Barker's Delight or The Art of Angling* provided the first truly coherent instructions for tying and fishing a modest assortment of some ten artificial flies, five general palmered patterns and five designed specifically to represent natural insects – mayflies, hawthorn flies, grasshoppers, oak flies (hover flies or saw flies?) and flesh flies (horseflies?). With his emphasis on the need to ensure that the fly alights before the line, and his observation that, 'now I work much of hogs wooll, for I finde it floateth best and procureth the best sport', Barker clearly recognized the merits of the dry fly, just as had Dame Juliana a century and a half earlier.

Izaak Walton, who first published his pastorally delightful but less than instructive work *The Compleat Angler* in 1653, was more of a bait fisher than a flyfisher, but his angling companion, Charles Cotton, who contributed an appendix to the fifth edition of the book, was essentially a flyfisher. A Derbyshire country squire, he fished the Dove for trout as a boy on his father's property at Beresford Hall on Derbyshire's border with Staffordshire, and later with Walton, his senior by some thirty-seven years, when he had inherited the family estate.

For all that their tackle may seem rudimentary today, it should not be thought that those who fished or wrote about fishing during the fifteenth, sixteenth and seventeenth centuries were unsophisticated. Indeed, Berners, Walton and Cotton all taught lessons too often ignored by modern anglers – dress unobtrusively; keep out of sight; match tackle and tactics to the season, the state of the water and the behaviour of the fish; and fish as fine as you sensibly can.

Tackle developed but slowly during the seventeenth and eighteenth centuries.

Horsehair lines inhibited adoption of that most obvious improvement, the reel, which was certainly in use in China in the late twelfth century, and possibly in Europe between the fourth and seventh centuries. The problem was that horsehair lines were knotted every two to three feet, preventing them from running freely through the rod rings that are so necessary an accompaniment to a reel. It was only with the gradual introduction of braided lines, either of silk or of a mixture of horsehair and silk, during the seventeenth century that the use of the reel became a practical proposition.

The first mention of a reel or 'winder' in an English angling book, albeit a somewhat cryptic one, is to be found in *Barker's Delight*. Even then, reels seem to have been slow to become widely accepted, not least, perhaps, because of the ease with which silk lines tangled. While some of them experimented with a variety of running-line contrivances – bobbins, frames not unlike those used for sea fishing hand-lines today, cleats and, the simplest of all expedients, the gathering of the line in the hand or on the ground – most anglers persevered for many years with lines fastened directly to their rod tips. It was not until the early nineteenth century that improvements in the quality of mixed silk and horsehair lines finally persuaded a growing majority of anglers to use them in preference to knotted horsehair.

Rods remained almost unchanged well into the nineteenth century. Certainly, they became longer (Cotton recommended one 15 to 18 feet long) and whole cane and whalebone were introduced – the former for middle joints and the latter to act as shock absorbers at the tip – but the principles of their construction and use were constant.

In the middle of the sixteenth century, catgut and (slightly later) silk-worm thread became known as possible alternatives to the length or two of horsehairs nearest to the fly. But although gut was stronger than horsehair, could be drawn finer and was less visible, it was scarcer, more difficult to tie secure knots with, soaked up water and then sank, and was found to rot more quickly, so relatively few people used it.

Dame Juliana's twelve fly patterns had burgeoned into some sixty-five listed by Cotton in his appendix to *The Compleat Angler* and continued to multiply at an extraordinary rate over the years thereafter. The vast majority of seventeenth- and eighteenth-century patterns were intended by those who dressed them to imitate or represent natural flies seen on the water. It was not really until the nineteenth century that attractor patterns began to come into their own – chiefly for sea trout but also for loch and river fishing for brown trout.

The predisposition towards the use of imitative patterns was reflected in the ways in which they were fished. There is some evidence to suggest that, rather than simply floating them on the surface until they became waterlogged and then being content to allow them to sink, anglers were increasingly and calculatedly fishing dry flies to trout that were rising and wet ones to those that were not. But they were still very much at the mercy of the wind. Their rods and lines made it difficult, or even impossible, to cast across the wind or into it, so they indulged almost exclusively in what was known as 'blow-line fishing', positioning themselves so as to allow the wind to carry their lines and flies to the fish, regardless of whether the fish were lying upstream or down.

One of the most difficult challenges facing modern angling historians is identification of the natural flies that ancient artificials were intended to represent. There seems to have been little or no general agreement about which fly was which, and the picture is further confused by evident general ignorance of matters entomological, and by the multitudes of local names by which particular species were known.

The first great step towards rectifying this – and thus towards enabling flyfishers to speak a common language – came in 1836 with the publication of Alfred Ronalds' *The Fly-Fisher's Entomology*.

It is difficult to over-state the importance of Ronalds' work. For the first time, he identified and catalogued almost all the natural flies that are of interest to fish and thus to fishermen, using a structured classification system, providing detailed and accurate drawings of each of the insects and similarly detailed drawings of artificials designed to represent them. The book laid the foundations for what was to amount to a complete revolution in fly-fishing over the next hundred years.

Five years later, in his *Vade Mecum of Fly Fishing for Trout*, first published in 1841, G.P.R. Pulman described dry-fly fishing thus:

> If the wet and heavy fly be exchanged for a dry and light one, and passed in artistic style over the feeding fish, it will, partly from the simple circumstances of its buoyancy, be taken, in nine cases out of ten, as greedily as the living insect itself.

It is on the basis of this passage that Pulman is generally regarded as the father of dry-fly fishing as we understand it today, but the choice between dry and wet fly was still heavily subject to the limitations of tackle and to the dictates of the wind.

After almost 300 years of near stagnation in terms of tackle design, the middle of the nineteenth century was a time of spectacular advances. Dressed silk lines – tapered, heavier and far less prone to tangling than anything that had gone before – became available, as did eyed hooks.

However good the floatants available, artificial flies eventually become waterlogged and sink, especially once fish have been caught on them.

The concept of the eyed hook had been around for centuries, and various people made and marketed them between the 1840s and 1870s, albeit without much success. It was not until the high-quality eyed trout hooks developed by H.S. Hall and George Bankart became available in 1879 that they began to gain wide acceptance. The new hooks made it possible to change flies quickly and easily – useful in all forms of fly-fishing but essential for dry-fly fishing – and the wire they were made from was fine enough for the tying of truly floating flies.

The final piece in the tackle development jigsaw that was to change the nature of fly-fishing for ever was the development of the built cane rod. In order fully to understand its significance, we need to cross the Atlantic. Details of the earliest fly-fishing in the United States are obscure, but the pursuit had clearly become established both for subsistence and for sport by the end of the seventeenth century. Early American flyfishers began by exploring East Coast rivers from Maine to Massachusetts. Over the next 200 years, fly-fishing followed in the wake of exploration of the continent, spreading to countless beautiful and prolific waters in its furthest flung corners – from Vermont and Virginia, to the Catskill Mountains of New York and the Poconos Mountains of Pennsylvania, way out to California, Oregon and Washington State. By 1860, even Montana and the remote and rugged Yellowstone plateau were surrendering their cutthroat trout to explorers, settlers and sportsmen.

Until the mid 1800s, and although they were increasingly designing flies to represent the naturals found on their rivers, the fly-fishing hardware used by American anglers – rods, reels, lines and hooks – mimicked that being made and used in Britain and, if anything, lagged slightly behind it. It was not until Hiram Leonard turned his hand from gun-making to rod-building in 1869 that this began to change.

Leonard's first rods were made from ash and lancewood, but it was not long before he was commissioned to build four-strip cane rods for Bradford & Anthony, a Boston sporting goods store. Ever innovative, he soon moved on to the sorts of six-strip rods we know today. Using a bevelling machine he had designed himself to cut the cane strips with extraordinary precision, working to carefully calculated mathematical formulae and using Tonkin cane while most others were still using inferior cane from Calcutta, he produced the lightest, most accurate and most beautiful rods the world had ever seen.

Overwhelmed with orders, Leonard took on a number of people who learnt their craft in his workshop and then went on to create their own successful businesses – Fred Thomas and Ed Payne among them.

Britain no longer led the world in tackle design; it followed in America's wake, struggling to keep up, and it was probably British anglers' patriotism rather than genuine public preference for their products that kept the British rod-making industry alive towards the end of the nineteenth century and into the twentieth.

These major innovations in lines, hooks and rods were to lead directly to fundamental changes in the ways in which people viewed their sport. The first had to do with specialization.

Hitherto, anglers had been anglers in the broadest sense of that word. No doubt some had preferred fly-fishing to legering or legering to float fishing, but the division between what we now call game and coarse fishing had been an ill-defined one. The records of such historic bodies as the Piscatorial Society and the Houghton Club show members to have been at least as interested in pike fishing as in fishing for trout or grayling until the mid 1800s. At Amwell Magna, one of the oldest fisheries in the country, members pursued pike, perch, roach and chub in preference to trout right up to the early 1900s.

It was the advances in fly tackle that created a clear division between coarse and game anglers within the space of a few years. For a while, it also gave fly-fishing something of an élitist image throughout the angling community and among the public at large. Fortunately, that was soon largely to be dispelled by the growth in popularity of still-water fly-fishing, which made the sport accessible to all.

The second consequence of these three major innovations was the growth of the dry-fly cult in the latter half of the nineteenth century. Drag – the skidding of a fly on the water's surface, caused by tension on fly-line and leader – however slight, is the greatest technical problem faced by the dry-flyfisher, and can best be overcome by casting upstream. The combination of the new, stiffer rods and heavier, more manageable lines freed flyfishers from the tyranny of the wind, enabling them to cast across it or even into it. They could cast upstream as and when they wished rather than merely when the wind decreed that they should; and the availability of eyed hooks enabled flyfishers to change their flies whenever necessary.

Quite suddenly, dry-fly fishing had became an entirely practical proposition. Not surprisingly, flyfishers pursued the new and exciting technique with great energy and enthusiasm, particularly on the chalk streams of southern England. The enthusiasm was fuelled and guided by the writings of a small number of articulate angling authors, F.M. Halford being foremost among them.

It can be argued – and I would not disagree – that chalk-stream fly-fishing would probably have developed much as it did without Halford's intervention.

Born of prosperous parents in 1844, his fly-fishing apprenticeship had been served between 1868 and 1877 on the River Wandle, at that time a pretty, pellucid stream with a fine head of fat, fussy trout. Dry-fly fishing was already common practice on it when Halford first trod its banks. By the late 1870s, creeping suburbia and increasingly frequent pollution were smothering the Wandle. In 1877, Halford joined the Houghton Fly Fishing Club on the Test, which had been formed a couple of years earlier and should not be confused with the neighbouring Houghton Club, established in 1822 and a rather more august institution. Because business commitments still tied him largely to London at that time, he continued to fish the Wandle for four more years before finally leaving to concentrate his attentions on the Hampshire chalk streams.

Degradation of the Wandle may not have been the only reason for Halford's piscatorial migration. In April 1879, a chance meeting with George Selwyn Marryat had sparked a friendship and a collaboration that were to last until Marryat's death in 1896. Marryat lived at Shedfield, just east of Southampton and within easy reach of Stockbridge, and it may well be that it was partly the development of this friendship that encouraged Halford to seek most of his sport on the Test.

It seems a little unfortunate that fate should have chosen Halford to become the standard bearer for the dry fly. Focused, dedicated and articulate he undoubtedly was, but it is difficult greatly to admire the other characteristics he brought to his self-appointed role.

Clearly, he saw himself as a researcher, studying trout and their diets. He spent countless hours analysing the contents of trouts' stomachs and examining natural flies in minute detail. But the essential characteristic of the truly capable scientist – an open mind and a willingness to listen to others – was signally lacking except, perhaps, in his relationship with his mentor, Marryat.

There were numerous other very experienced and knowledgeable chalk-stream flyfishers around and many of them became friends of Halford. Any or all of them could have brought balance to Halford's work but, while he spent much time in their company, usually discussing fish and fishing, he appears to have learnt remarkably little from them. Following publication of his first book, *Floating Flies and How to Dress Them*, in 1886, and then *Dry Fly Fishing in Theory and Practice* in 1889, he seems increasingly to have believed himself to be the fount of all knowledge on such subjects, enjoying the guru status they gave him and holding court rather than engaging in discussion.

Halford's relationship with Marryat differed greatly from his relationships with other anglers. The collaboration between the two men in preparing *Floating Flies* was very close, but it cannot be said that they brought equal and complementary talents to their work. Marryat stood head and shoulders above Halford.

Rated by many as the greatest flyfisher in England, Marryat was a gifted entomologist and a great observer of nature with a remarkable capacity for thinking himself into the fishes' minds. He was pragmatic, experimental and innovative, and there is strong circumstantial evidence – not least from his fly boxes – that he was liberal in his approach to fly-fishing and certainly no dry-fly purist.

Given the closeness of their relationship, it is interesting that Marryat declined to be cited with Halford as co-author of *Floating Flies*. There has been much speculation about why this should have been. Some have attributed it to his reserved nature. Marryat was no limelight seeker and he greatly disliked flattery, although Halford's tribute to him in the preface to the book could scarcely have been more fulsome. It is quite possible that natural reticence was his primary reason for declining to be identified as co-author, but one cannot but wonder whether he may not also have been a little uncomfortable with Halford's growing preoccupation with the dry fly and with exact imitation.

Had Halford been prepared to listen to others and had he been a more intellectually agile thinker, he might have come to realize the fundamental flaws in his arguments – the irrationality of seeking to represent the winged insects trout eat but not the nymphs of those same insects; the absurdity of seeking to imitate flies precisely, and the even greater absurdity of designing them from a human viewpoint rather than from the trout's; and the folly of seeking to imitate every winged fly trout eat. He might even have become more rather than less tolerant. As it was, once he had reached a conclusion, that conclusion – right or wrong – became gospel, and he would studiously avoid being drawn into any discussion of it.

Apologists for Halford often claim that he himself was no dry-fly purist but that it was his followers who seized on his ideas and carried them to extremes. That is untrue. It is perfectly clear that as time went on Halford himself came truly to believe that the dry fly was the only respectable means of taking chalk-stream trout and that all other methods were beyond the pale. Those of his supporters who quote from his works to demonstrate his tolerance of wet-fly fishing almost always do so out of context. Look up anything he wrote acknowledging the worth of the wet fly, read on from it, and you will invariably come across a literal or metaphorical 'but . . .'.

It is interesting, too, that Halford was not even a particularly skilful flyfisher. His catches were consistently modest by any standards and the more so when it is realized that his views on chalk-stream fishery management had chiefly to do with tipping in large numbers of farm-reared fish, even into waters with thriving populations of wild trout.

So, why was Halford so influential – why were his idiosyncratic and often irrational views so widely accepted and adopted by flyfishers and fishery owners alike? From the angler's perspective, the answer is almost certainly that he was the only person writing copiously about the subject during a period of dramatic change. From the fishery owner's point of view, it may have had to do, in part at least, with the way in which changes in society were putting increasing pressure on chalk-stream fisheries.

The arrival of the train in the nineteenth century, combined with increasing affluence and leisure time, led to a dramatic growth in angling pressure on waters of all sorts, and trout streams were no exception. Whereas hitherto, dons and undergraduates from Oxford had made something of an expedition of riding out to Fairford to spend a weekend fishing the Colne, now, quite suddenly, individuals and groups of flyfishers could board a train at Waterloo on a Saturday morning, be on the water on the Test or the Itchen by ten and be back in London by bedtime, having fished the evening rise. Similar excursions were becoming increasingly practicable throughout the United Kingdom and it was not long before the motor car made fishing even more accessible.

This stretching of the supply-and-demand equation has been resolved – albeit on an *ad hoc* basis rather than through some grand scheme – by limiting access to rivers, by increasing the capacity of the rivers themselves to accommodate anglers and by turning increasing numbers of stillwaters into trout fisheries to cater for the overflow.

A long-established tradition of riparian ownership, especially in England, provided the key to limitation of access. As more and more people began to seek fishing, so increasingly did proprietors of stretches of water begin to recognize the value of their assets, and to let rods on them or to lease them to syndicates or clubs. Inevitably, prices rose, particularly on good water in densely populated areas, and very soon the cost of fishing a chalk stream in southern England had outstripped most anglers' pockets. Elsewhere, most notably in Scotland and Ireland but also in Wales and in the north and west of England, where fishing pressure has been lighter than in the south-east, the gap between supply and demand has remained narrower, so access has been less restricted and the cost of fishing has been held at more modest levels.

As the demand for fishing has grown, so has fishery owners' and managers' concern for their fisheries and their fish stocks. The imposition of a 'dry fly only' rule places significant constraints on anglers, reducing pressure on the water and limiting opportunities for taking fish, which suits riparian owners well.

The significance of Halford's influence should not be underestimated. It is echoed to this day in the imposition by most chalk-stream fisheries of 'upstream only' rules and, by some, of rules that allow only dry-fly fishing until midsummer with the use of nymphs being permitted thereafter, sometimes somewhat grudgingly. More generally and more importantly, the so-called 'imitative' fly-fishing techniques that evolved during Halford's time and thereafter have had profound influences on fly-fishing methods wherever they are practised, on waters running, still or salt, world-wide.

It fell to G.E.M. Skues to rationalize chalk-stream fly-fishing, and a long, uphill job he had of it. Skues, born fourteen years after Halford, could scarcely have contrasted with him more starkly.

A Winchester scholar, Skues began fly-fishing on the college's water on the Itchen in 1874 and then, following a pause after leaving school in 1877, fished chiefly at Abbotts Barton, immediately upstream from the college water, for fifty-six years, from 1883 to 1938. A lawyer by profession, his writing was very different from Halford's, being as notable for its wit as for its wisdom.

Skues was a superb flyfisher – observant, analytical, adaptable and inventive. He caught extraordinary numbers of trout and his concerns about over-stocking contributed to his decision eventually to resign his rod at Abbotts Barton.

Skues' reservations about Halford's views developed quite gradually. In the foreword to his first book, *Minor Tactics of the Chalk Stream*, published in 1910, he describes Halford's *Dry Fly Fishing in Theory and Practice* as '. . . the greatest work, in my opinion, which has ever seen the light on the subject of angling for trout and grayling.'

The twenty-one years that separated publication of *Dry Fly Fishing* and *Minor Tactics* had not been uneventful. Halford and Skues had first met in 1891. Sponsored by Halford and William Senior, Skues had joined The Flyfishers' Club in 1893, and by 1897 had joined Halford and other luminaries on the club's committee. Halford had written *Making a Fishery*, published in 1895, and *An Angler's Autobiography*, published in 1903.

Through astute observation, Skues had become aware of the importance of nymphs in trouts' diets as early as 1888. The following year, he had written a letter to *The Field* advocating the use of a wet fly fished upstream when chalk-stream trout were not surface feeding. By 1908 at the very latest, he had begun replacing the conventional wet flies in his fly box with artificials designed specifically to represent nymphs. In the interests of balance, it must be said that throughout this period – and for the rest of his life – Skues was a pragmatist rather than a rebel, fascinated by and taking great satisfaction from dry-fly fishing but always being prepared to play the fish at their own game, offering them sub-surface patterns when they were taking sub-surface food.

Given that his ideas on nymph fishing were quite well developed by the time *Minor Tactics* was published, it seems strange that so important a book should have been almost exclusively about wet-fly fishing, with no more than five pages devoted to nymph fishing.

It was this focus on the wet fly that gave Halford and his disciples the opportunity to perpetuate the myth that nymph fishing and wet-fly fishing were one and the same, to protest about the inefficiency of and the damage done by fishing wet flies across and down – wilfully ignoring all Skues said about casting upstream to seen, feeding fish – and, for good measure, to put forward specious arguments about the impracticability of imitating nymphs' movements.

When Halford died in 1914, he left behind him a retinue of staunch supporters with whom Skues was to be in dispute for much of the rest of his life – a dispute that caused him considerable frustration, leading to a vigorous but inconclusive debate at The Flyfishers' Club in 1938 and to the publication of his *Nymph Fishing for Chalk Stream Trout* the following year.

When Skues died in 1949, many flyfishers still clung to the view that dry-fly fishing was the only 'sporting' way in which to catch chalk-stream trout and that nymph fishing was, at best, a tactic to be used furtively on particularly difficult days in high summer and, at worst, cheating. Fortunately, Skues had already passed on his baton to Frank Sawyer, an immensely experienced, observant and respected river keeper on the Wiltshire Avon, along with the introductions that were to enable Sawyer to promote his views in print and on radio and television.

Whereas Skues had produced a whole range of nymphs designed to imitate the naturals, Sawyer relied on just two – the Pheasant Tail Nymph and the Grey Goose Nymph – as generally representative patterns; and he caused a certain amount of consternation among the chalk-stream traditionalists by weighting them with wire. But so obviously perceptive and knowledgeable was Sawyer, and so firmly had the validity of nymph fishing become established by Skues' work, that the carping was short-lived and most river flyfishers embraced his teachings enthusiastically. As a result, and although there are still some fisheries that impose a 'dry fly only' rule for at least part of the season, nymph fishing has become generally accepted as an entirely proper means of taking fish feeding below the water's surface.

While chalk-stream anglers were going their own esoteric way during the late nineteenth century and the first half of the twentieth, flyfishers in other parts of the United Kingdom were developing and refining their own styles and techniques.

In the Borders and in the north of England, perhaps the most skilful of all fly-fishing methods, the upstream wet fly, was being perfected, with tiny, delicate spider patterns, often in teams of two or three, being cast upstream on short lines. It had, in fact, become quite well developed by the early 1800s, but it was an Edinburgh lawyer, W.C. Stewart, who was eventually to write one of the definitive works on the subject, *The Practical Angler*, published in 1857. Well ahead of his colleagues in the south, he was the first writer to emphasize the benefits of fishing upstream.

Stewart's book was aptly titled. He was, indeed, a very practical angler and he wrote compellingly, but he did not seek to catalogue large numbers of wet flies or truly to codify upstream wet-fly fishing. That was for T.E. Pritt to do twenty-eight years later in his *Yorkshire Trout Flies*, published in 1885. As well as describing various north country styles of wet-fly fishing, Pritt included over sixty patterns collected from Yorkshire anglers. Perhaps concerned by the apparent parochialism of the book's title, the second edition, published in 1886, was re-titled *North Country Flies*.

On spate rivers in Wales, north-west England and in Scotland, attractor patterns such as the Alexandra, the Butcher and the Peter Ross were coming into their own, fished across and downstream. In the north and in the south-west of England, in Wales and on the great rivers of eastern Scotland, those who were not engaged in the pursuit of salmon fished pragmatically for trout and sea trout, borrowing dry-fly techniques from the chalk-stream flyfishers, using upstream wet flies as they saw fit and fishing across and down with attractor patterns, chiefly for sea trout at night.

The twentieth century was a period of consolidation and refinement, rather than of dramatic change.

Nylon monofilament, introduced in the late 1940s, became widely accepted as a significant improvement on gut for leaders. Fine, clear and relatively strong, it needed no soaking to make it supple as gut did and, provided one remembered to store it in the dark and to renew one's supplies every year or two, it was – and is – reasonably reliable. More recently, we have seen the arrival of several variations on the monofilament theme. First came double-strength leader material, and then fluorocarbon and copolymer monofilaments, both of which are claimed to offer advantages over more traditional nylon in terms of both invisibility and strength for a given thickness. We shall discuss them in Chapter 4.

Dressed silk fly-lines were superseded by synthetic ones from the mid 1950s onwards, leading to the development of an extraordinary multiplicity of fly-line profiles and densities. Fibreglass made a size-able dent in the built cane rod market in the 1960s and had itself been almost completely replaced by carbon fibre by the end of the 1970s. Reels have become lighter, and large arbor versions, introduced in the 1990s, are markedly more efficient than their predecessors. The use of synthetics for fly-tying and improvements in hook design and manufacture have also contributed to significant developments in trout-fly design.

Increasing international travel and rapidly improving communications during the past thirty years or so have broadened flyfishers' horizons enormously. Anglers of many nationalities have been brought into contact with philosophies, fly patterns and fishing techniques developed elsewhere, adapting them for use on their home waters. There are countless examples, perhaps the most dramatic being the way in which catch-and-release – common practice in America – has become recognized world-wide as an effective tool for the management of wild trout populations. In Britain, nymph patterns and nymph-fishing techniques developed in Poland and the Czech Republic have been widely adopted, as have fly patterns originating from Scandinavia, the United States and even the Netherlands, home to a number of remarkably innovative fly dressers.

Intriguing as many of them are, all of these things are really only refinements rather than fundamental changes in the ways in which we fish. While they may make our sport more interesting, a little easier and a bit more fun, there is not much that is very radical about them. In truth, the basics of fly-fishing – the putting of an artificial fly to a fish with rod and line – have changed very little in the two thousand years of the sport's recorded history.

2   Where and What For?

From stately southern chalk streams through the pretty tranquillity of the limestone rivers of Derbyshire and Gloucestershire and the torrents that tumble east and west from the Pennines before meandering sedately to the sea, to the sometimes peat-stained becks, brooks and rivers of Northern Ireland, Scotland, Wales and the West Country, British flyfishers have access to a remarkable variety of streams and rivers.

The characteristics of any stream or river are governed by the nature of the land over or through which its water flows, and the river's characteristics govern the fish it will sustain. If we understand these relationships, it is usually possible to predict quite accurately the species and sizes of fish that will be found in a particular water, how they may be expected to behave and the sorts of tackle, flies and tactics that are most likely to be effective.

Small, infertile streams support small trout (or no fish at all); more fertile rivers support larger trout and, quite often, grayling, dace, chub, perch and pike. In their lower reaches, where they are more sluggish, less well aerated and often prone to silting, rivers usually support coarse fish rather than trout, although sea trout may well pass through on their way up from the sea to spawn.

Almost all streams and rivers of any size change in character between their sources and their estuaries or the points at which they join other watercourses. Most obviously, the speed of the water drops and the size of a stream grows as the valley through which it flows flattens out and tributaries join it. But other, more complicated, factors have roles to play, too.

As water runs through or over rock, it absorbs dissolved mineral salts which fertilize it. The softer the rock, the more easily is it dissolved, particularly if the water spends a substantial period of time in contact with it. Chalk and, to a lesser extent, sandstone and limestone are soft and readily dissolved; granite is hard and yields almost no salts at all – which is why chalk and limestone streams produce luxuriant weed growth and big trout, while rivers running off granite mountains produce little weed and small trout.

The vegetation in the water catchment areas can also significantly influence the nature of a stream. Where rainwater seeps into a watercourse through peat or decaying bracken, heather or pine needles, the stream will usually have a brownish tinge, often quite dark, which excludes light and thus inhibits weed growth, and its water will be acidic.

Man, that inveterate meddler, has altered the characters of most of our rivers. Some have been dammed to form reservoirs from which water is drawn for domestic and industrial use, reducing water levels and obstructing the passage of migratory fish.

Boreholes are used to abstract water from aquifers, the underground reservoirs that feed many of our finest rivers, reducing water levels and flow rates in the rivers themselves. Such reductions in the volume of water inevitably increase concentrations of pollutants unless the quantities of pollutants are reduced.

In the middle and lower reaches of many rivers, 'improved' land drainage has sharply increased the speed at which water levels rise and fall in response to rainfall. Draconian dredging and weed cutting, done solely to improve drainage, can turn attractive and productive streams into dull, largely lifeless canals.

Lastly, man has, of course, developed an astonishing array of techniques for polluting rivers, from sewage and industrial and chemical effluent through the seepage of fertilizers, herbicides, pesticides and agricultural waste to run-off from dirty, oily roads and the accidental spillage of petrol, oil, creosote, and other poisons. Agricultural fertilizers significantly increase the fertility of some rivers, invariably to their detriment. Algae and blanket weed choking a watercourse benefit neither fish nor fisherman. Other forms of pollution de-oxygenate the water, killing fish and other animal life by suffocation, sometimes for very considerable distances downstream. In the worst cases, once-lovely trout streams have been bled almost dry by abstraction and then simply poisoned with all manner of waste until they have become nothing more than noxious and unsightly open sewers. In some cases, they now dry up in summer or have even disappeared altogether.

But the purpose of this chapter is to examine the many marvellous rivers that remain rather than to bemoan those that have gone, and not all of the work done by man has been detrimental. Indeed, some – especially on the chalk streams, but on some other waters, too – has greatly benefited the fish and, therefore, the angler. Hatches and weirs, usually built for purposes other than simply to improve a fishery, oxygenate the water and encourage it to carve out deep pools, providing ideal holding areas for trout and grayling. Bridges provide shade and shelter, which is why it always pays to approach them cautiously and fish them carefully.

The essential difference between a chalk stream or brook and other burns, becks and rivers lies in their respective sources and in the nature of the land over which they flow.

Chalk Streams

Chalk is highly permeable and rain falling on to it soaks straight into it, as into a sponge, rather than simply running off. As the water sinks down through the chalk, it is filtered and then settles into the water table or aquifer. In section, the aquifer is domed rather than having a flat surface like a lake. The dome rises and falls through the year in response to rainfall, being at its highest in early spring, after the winter's downpours, and at its lowest towards the end of the summer. Throughout its time in the aquifer, the water is absorbing salts from the chalk and becoming increasingly fertile.

As the dome rises, its surface reaches points of weakness in the ground and the water pours out, running away as a stream. Not unnaturally, the springs lowest in the water table are the earliest to break and the last to fail. Some, below the point where the top of the water table never falls, never fail. Others, high up, break late and always fail by July or August. Streams fed by such predictably fallible springs are termed 'winterbournes'.

Rivers fed by chalk springs make ideal trout fisheries. Their water is clear, which enables us to see the fish – and the fish to see us. They rise and fall very little in response to rain because the water tends to soak into the chalk rather than run straight off it, which means that the rivers remain fishable almost regardless of the weather. They are extremely fertile and therefore sustain large quantities of weed, which in turn sustains insect life, which in turn produces big, healthy fish – and some problems.

Weed cutting is hard work for river keepers, and to cut weed properly is a considerable craft. The objects are to provide open lies for the fish and fishable water for the fisherman, and to maintain the flow of the water while at the same time leaving sufficient weed to provide prolific larders for the trout. It is important that weed, such as starwort that encourages silting should be removed, and that weeds, such as ranunculus and water celery, that provide excellent shelter for the creatures trout eat and do not accumulate mud should just be given judicious haircuts.

On major chalk streams such as the Test, the Itchen, the Kennet and the Wylye, and the Driffield Beck in Yorkshire, river keepers agree weed-cutting dates before the season opens and they all cut their weed at the same time. With great rafts of weed floating down on their currents, the rivers can be effectively unfishable on weed-cutting days and for a day or so thereafter, and a well-publicized programme enables anglers to avoid the irritation thus caused. On small chalk brooks, it is usually possible to run a net from bank to bank, cut a stretch immediately upstream of it and then haul out the weed. This obviates the need for a co-ordinated programme on those rivers where the job is usually done by busy riparian owners, rather than by full-time professional keepers.

Spate Rivers

Spate rivers are far more variable in character than chalk streams, the quality of their water being a direct product of the ground on which they rise and over which they run, but they all have one thing in common. Although some are augmented by springs or lakes, they are all either largely or exclusively fed by rainwater running off the land. As a consequence, they tend to rise and fall very quickly in response to rainfall, or the lack of it, and to be innately infertile because the bedrock is hard, containing few soluble mineral salts, and because they are in direct contact with it relatively briefly.

The rapid rise and fall of a spate river is significant. When the water is low, its banks and the beds of the streams and rivulets feeding it dry out and accumulate an assortment of wind-borne bits and pieces – leaves, twigs, dust and loose soil. When the rain comes, it washes all this material down the watercourse, the river becoming coloured and, usually, unfishable.

Spates can also be hazardous to anglers, rivers rising very rapidly with little or no warning. The fisherman wading on midstream shallows that may have been readily accessible when the water was low can find himself cut off from the bank surprisingly easily, and a few flyfishers are actually swept away by flash floods each year.

Fertility

The fertility of a stream or river – or its infertility – is important to the angler, not only because it has a direct effect on the species and sizes of the fish that live in it and the varieties and quantities of the creatures they live on, but also because it influences the behaviour of the trout and the ways in which they feed. At opposite ends of the scale, in a chalk stream or in a fertile spate river such as the Eden, luxuriant weed beds may be found across the whole width of the river. The trout take up lies among them and in the gaps between them, which means that they may be found almost anywhere. With a mass of food to choose from, they grow large; they can afford to be selective and often are. In contrast, infertile streams, such as the headwaters of most spate rivers and major rivers such as the Teign in Devonshire and the Swale in Yorkshire, are sparse in weed. The trout that live in them take up lies wherever they can find refuge from the current, shade in summer and protection from predators – ahead of and behind rocks and boulders, by groynes and fallen branches, under overhanging trees and bushes and in the slack water beneath steep, cut-away banks. With food in short supply, they are very often small and free-rising, and they may be relatively unselective.

The Quarry

So we come to the fish themselves. Those that inhabit British rivers and may be taken on artificial flies are brown trout, sea trout, grayling and rainbow trout. Several species of coarse fish can be taken on artificial flies, too, but they are rarely the flyfisher's primary quarry and we shall not therefore consider them in any detail.

Brown trout, sea trout and grayling are indigenous to Britain and are found wild in many British rivers. In heavily fished rivers, wild brown trout often have to share the water with farm-reared ones and sometimes with rainbow trout, imported from the west coast of the United States towards the end of the nineteenth century and now reared in almost all British trout farms.

All of these fish have certain characteristics in common, especially in terms of their life histories, feeding, eyesight and senses of hearing, smell and taste, so I shall consider our primary quarry, brown trout and sea trout, in detail first and then go on to examine the specific attributes of grayling, rainbow trout and coarse fish.

Brown Trout and Sea Trout (*Salmo trutta*)

It may seem strange to group brown trout and sea trout together but they are, in fact, one and the same species – *Salmo trutta*. In the interests of clarity, I shall refer throughout this book to those trout that do not migrate as brown trout and those that do as sea trout, but it is important to understand that there is, in reality, absolutely no difference between them apart from the fact that some of them elect to remain in freshwater while others choose to spend parts of their lives in estuaries or in the sea.

With their innate sense of order, human beings find it difficult to accept that the four-to-the-pound brown trout they see in moorland brooks and the portly, bronzed and vermilion-spotted aldermen of the Test are no different in any way from the glittering silver sea trout that run up our rivers to spawn, having spent months or years in saltwater. They find it even more difficult to accept that every brown trout has a migratory instinct and that brown trout that fail to migrate do so only because they find themselves in surroundings comfortable enough to make migration unnecessary, or because they find themselves land-locked and are therefore denied the opportunity to migrate.

Nineteenth-century taxonomists delighted in identifying and naming new species and sub-species of fish, usually on evidence as superficial as markings, coloration or slight variations in habit. In the mid 1800s, there were supposed to be at least ten separate species of brown trout in Britain alone, including croneen, dollaghan, gillaroo, Great Lake trout, sewin, finnock, ferox trout, Loch Leven trout, and Galway and Orkney sea trout, all of them dignified with distinctive taxonomic names.

In the twentieth century, all brown and sea trout were increasingly recognized as a single species, variations in appearance or habit being no more than local adaptations to environmental circumstances. Only recently, though, has it become clear that every brown trout has the capacity to become a sea trout and that any male brown trout, migratory or not, can fertilize the ova of any female brown trout or sea trout. This is not interbreeding as some have suggested, implying the cross-breeding of two separate species. It is perfectly normal mating between two fish of the same species.

Genetic studies of sea trout carried out by the eminent Irish fisheries biologists Dr Ken Whelan and Professor Andy Ferguson have shown that the sea trout's migratory behaviour is almost certainly an inherited trait passed down the generations through the mitochondrial DNA – non-nuclear DNA, which is inherited only through the female line without crossing-over. If this is so, it may well account for the marked preponderance of females among those trout that go to sea.

Perhaps the most remarkable characteristic of the salmonids, and the one that confused taxonomists and biologists for so long, is their adaptability. They are extraordinarily adept at adjusting their coloration to provide them with the best possible camouflage. Their digestive systems adapt quite quickly to locally available food – one group of brown trout in Ireland has been found to have a markedly thicker stomach lining than the norm, to accommodate the snails that make up a significant proportion of their diet. And they have a remarkable ability to move easily from saltwater to fresh and back again. Dr Ken Whelan has shown that brown trout from high-altitude hill loughs in the west of Ireland retain their ability to live in saltwater despite the fact that their ancestors cannot have experienced saltwater conditions for many thousands of years.

Further evidence of the migratory nature of trout is to be found in the habits of brown trout living in all sorts of waters. Examples are to be seen in large Irish and Scottish lakes – Loughs Melvin and Neagh and Lochs Awe, Ericht and Rannoch. Many of the trout born in such lakes' feeder streams migrate into the lakes themselves to grow and mature, running back up the streams to spawn – behaving exactly like sea trout. It is clearly of no concern to them that the 'seas' in which they spend substantial parts of their lives consist of freshwater rather than salt.

The fact that brown trout and sea trout are one and the same is of profound importance. It means that wherever the species is introduced into river systems, there is a potential for sea-trout runs to develop, whatever the ancestry of the stock, as has happened in Canada, the United States, Patagonia, the Falkland Islands, Tasmania and New Zealand. It also offers real hope for rivers in which sea trout have become scarce. Provided a viable brown-trout population remains, sea-trout runs may be expected to build again naturally when the problems that caused the decline have been rectified.

The Brown Trout's Life Cycle

British brown trout spawn in the winter, between November and February. For reasons we do not fully understand, stocked, farm-reared brown trout rarely spawn as successfully as wild trout and quite often fail to survive their first winter in the river. That is not a matter for great regret. Where farm-reared brown trout breed with wild ones, there is always a risk of dilution of essential genetic characteristics of successful wild trout populations. Increasingly, this risk is being reduced by allowing river fisheries to stock only with triploid brown trout – fish genetically modified to have three sets of chromosomes instead of the normal two, rendering them sterile.

Trout need clean, reasonably fast-flowing, well-oxygenated streams and rivers in which to spawn. In anticipation of spawning, they move into stretches with loose gravel beds through which the water can percolate, washing the eggs. These areas, known as redds, are often some distance upstream from the areas in which non-migratory brown trout live during the rest of the year.

On a redd, a hen fish cuts a hollow in the gravel with sweeps of her tail and then lays some of the several hundred ova she is carrying into it. Simultaneously, her mate, holding position beside and usually very slightly ahead of her, discharges a stream of milt into the current, some of it reaching and fertilizing the ova. The hen fish then moves a foot or so upstream and cuts another hollow, the pebbles washed out of it covering the fertilized ova in the previous one and thus protecting them.

Mating, although not usually fatal, is a debilitating process and the fish may need as long as two or three months to regain condition, which is why the trout season is generally closed from the end of October until the middle of April – although the opening date is extremely variable, ranging from the middle of January on some Scottish rivers to the beginning of May on one or two chalk streams. A few of the older trout may be unable to compete with the younger ones especially in rivers sparse in food, and fail to regain weight lost in spawning. Such fish, readily identifiable by their gauntness, even when caught in June or July, are best compassionately dispatched, although they will be unfit to eat.

After about four to twelve weeks in the redds, depending on the water temperature, the ova hatch into alevins, strange, almost tadpole-like creatures, which continue to live for some time on yolk sacs hanging from their throats. As the yolk sacs become depleted, the alevins become increasingly fish-like and are soon clearly identifiable as fry.

The fry live in shoals in slack water, usually close to the shore, and feed on the minute invertebrates they find there. They, in turn, provide easy pickings for a whole range of predators and the mortality rate from the oval stage until the young fish are big enough to be reasonably safe is staggeringly high. Even when fully grown, trout continue to be preyed upon by herons, otters, mink and pike.

At first sight, small brown trout are very similar in appearance to salmon parr, and it is important to be able to differentiate between the two. The most obvious distinguishing features are:

Brown trout	**Salmon parr**
Upper lip extends to the rear edge of the (relatively small) eye	Upper lip extends to the middle of the (relatively large) eye
Tail fin slightly forked with rounded lobes	Tail fin deeply forked with pointed lobes
Adipose, pectoral and pelvic fins pinky orange	Adipose, pectoral and pelvic fins grey

Unlike most warm-blooded creatures including man, the sizes to which trout grow are very largely dependent on water temperature and on the amount of food available to them. On average, wild brown trout in fertile chalk streams, such as the Test, the Itchen and the Kennet, grow to about 12 inches during the first three years of their lives while those in infertile rain-fed rivers such as the Dart, the Tamar and the North Esk, grow to only about 5 or 6 inches during the same period.

In exceptionally favourable circumstances, brown trout may grow to 20 pounds or more. The current rod-caught record is held by a fish of 31 pounds 12 ounces taken from Loch Awe in 2002. That non-migratory fish was over 3 pounds heavier than the record 28 pounds 5 ounces sea trout taken from Calshot Spit on the River Test estuary in 1992.

Feeding

There is a myth, probably started by the chalk-stream pundits of the late nineteenth century, that trout, particularly chalk-stream trout, live exclusively on genteel diets of mayflies, pale wateries and iron blue duns. Nothing could be further from the truth. Trout are simply carnivorous predators, feeding on any living creature small enough, palatable enough and accessible enough for them to eat.

The old adage that 'you are what you eat' is even truer in fish than in humans. Most people grow to a predictable size, within quite narrow limits, almost regardless of how much or how little they eat. Some families of fish, including the salmonids, are different. Although there are evident limits to eventual total size, they generally adapt their sizes to the amount of food available. That is why healthy, mature trout in infertile waters may weigh no more than a few ounces while their relatives in more fertile waters, and those that go to sea to feed, may weigh several pounds – exceptionally, as much as 10, 20 or even 30 pounds.

A trout's chief objective is to acquire enough protein to enable it to thrive and grow, and to do this with the least possible expenditure of effort. To this end, it will take nymphs and sedge and stonefly larvae from the stream or river bed, snails, nymphs and freshwater shrimps from among the weed, fry of all sorts from the marginal shallows and terrestrial insects – ants, gnats, hawthorn flies, caterpillars, beetles, daddy-long-legs and moths – that fall or are blown on to the water from overhanging trees and bushes and from surrounding fields and hedgerows, just as cheerfully as they will take nymphs ascending to hatch and adult up-winged flies and sedges.

Some anglers tend to be disparaging about so-called cannibal trout, apparently believing them to be almost a separate species from the brown trout they take on fly, or necessarily old and grizzly. In truth, all trout eat fish smaller than themselves from time to time, and a few become largely or exclusively piscivorous – usually because they have grown too big to be sustained by the insect and other invertebrate food forms available to them. Apart from this, these 'cannibals' are no different from any other brown trout.

It is, of course, impossible to quantify the proportions of their food that trout take from the surface or beneath it; the figures vary widely from water to water. But I am quite certain that on most rivers, and especially on the most fertile ones, as much as 85 per cent is taken well below the surface.

The fishes' feeding habits are chiefly dictated by the temperature of the water and by the availability of food. Brown trout and grayling will feed when the water temperature is between 8° and 15°C and do so most enthusiastically when it is between 10° and 13°C. They can survive in water between about 0° and 20°C provided it is sufficiently well oxygenated, but become increasingly torpid as the temperature approaches either of these extremes. Rainbow trout prefer slightly higher temperatures, feeding most enthusiastically in water at between 12° and 16°C and being able to survive temperatures of up to about 24°C, which, incidentally, is why they generally do rather better than brown trout in lowland lakes, which can become warm in summer.

Early in the season, when the water is cold, the fish tend to stay close to the bottom and to feed, when they feed at all, on such food forms as may be available to them there. As both the water and the air warm up through April, May and early June, the trout will take advantage of the increasing variety of insects available to them, culminating on some rivers, especially in Ireland and in the south of England, with the mayfly hatch, which runs, fairly predictably, from mid May until the end of the second week in June.

Thereafter, fly hatches tend to fall off, and much of the trout's food during the dog days of July and August is found among the weed, chiefly in the form of nymphs and freshwater shrimps. On overcast days, when the air is still or when there is a light south-westerly breeze, there may be hatches of iron blue duns or pale wateries during the day, and the fish may rise to them. Falls of spinners or hatches of sedges just before dusk may produce spectacular, if often challenging, evening rises.

It is not until September, when both the air and the water start to cool again, that hatches of up-winged flies will produce a flurry of surface feeding before the brown trout season closes at the end of the month or in October.

Eyesight

A trout's eyes, set on either side of its head, have only a fairly narrow
field of binocular vision, but provide the fish with a very wide monoc-
ular arc, which enables it to spot prey out of the corner of its eye and to
take heed of potential danger. The blind arc behind a trout is quite
narrow – no more than about 25 or 30 degrees, but awareness of it can
make it easier for the angler to approach a fish unobserved.

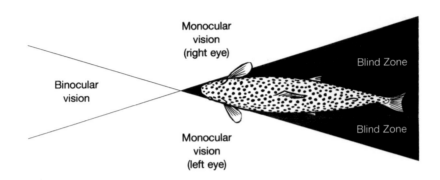

Fig. 1 The trout's fields of vision

There is no doubt that trout can identify colours in very much the same
range as those we see, but probably leaning towards the red end of the
spectrum and possibly including one or two frequencies beyond the
range of the human eye. If the flyfisher learns nothing else about the
trout's senses, it is essential that he or she should at least develop a
working understanding of the way in which fish see things in, on and
above the water. All freshwater fish depend very heavily on their
eyesight to warn them of impending danger, and most of them –
particularly the predators – rely almost exclusively on it for the identification and taking of food items. Because the ways in which light
behaves in air and in water are very different, the fish's visual perceptions of his surroundings are quite unlike ours.

Three factors cause these differences – reflection from the water's surface, refraction i.e. the way in which light bends as it passes from air into water, and colour absorption i.e. the way in which various colours are progressively filtered out as light passes down through the water. Colour absorption is of greatest significance to the stillwater angler, who often works his fly or lure at far greater depths than the stream or river flyfisher does, but reflection and refraction are important to us all.

Light striking the water's surface at 90 degrees penetrates well and passes straight down into it. As the angle of attack is reduced, so is the light's penetrating power, more and more of it being reflected back off the water. The light that does get through is refracted (bent) down-wards. At an angle of attack of about 20 degrees, by far the greater part of the light is being reflected and the small amount that does get through is being refracted downwards at an angle of about 40 degrees. At 10 degrees and less, no light penetrates the surface at all.

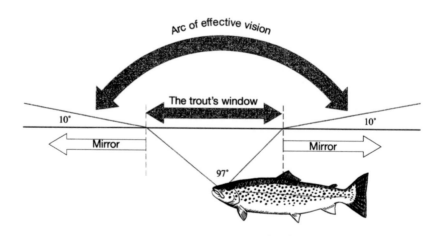

Fig. 2 The trout's window

The effect of all this is that a fish sees the underside of the water's surface as a mirror in which are reflected the things around him and in the centre of which, immediately above him, is a circular hole or window, through which he can see the outside world. Because the light's ability to penetrate the surface decreases gradually as the angle of attack is reduced, rather than simply stopping abruptly, the edge of the window is ill defined. The window for a fish lying deep in the water is larger than that for one lying close to the surface.

The immediate importance of this to the angler lies in the extent to which the fish can or cannot see him (and his rod) and the extent to which he may be able to use the blind area outside the fish's window to conceal himself. But there is far more to it than that.

In calm water, an unbroken mirror surrounding the fish's window affords a constant and, presumably, reassuring background to his life. Floating food forms borne towards him on the current appear initially as indentations in the mirror. It is evident from their behaviour that trout learn to interpret these indentations. While it is still quite clearly beyond his window, a trout will start to lift in the water to intercept a natural fly, even apparently identifying a particular species on which he is feeding some time before he can see its body or wings. Thereafter, because of refraction, the fly's wings will appear in the trout's window, seemingly detached from the insect's body and suspended in the air. Only when the fly's legs and feet appear in the window will the fish at last be able to see it as a complete entity. By this time, he has usually risen to meet it and is almost, but not quite, committed to taking it.

From this it is evident that the initial impressions our flies make on the trout are important, and that his view of a fly is likely to be very different from our own, the feet and wings being of primary significance.

The way in which a trout sees our fly-line and leader is of considerable importance, too. A floating fly-line and a length of floating nylon both appear in the mirror like great hawsers across the sky; they look much bigger than they actually are because of the sizeable dent each makes in the surface film. If they are moved – when being retrieved, for example, or when being lifted off to be recast – they cause far more disturbance than may be evident from above the water. Obviously, all of this has serious implications in terms of our tackle's fish-frightening capabilities.

Hearing
The trout's next line of defence after his eyesight is his hearing. Most fish do have vestigial or rudimentary ears, concealed beneath the skin at the backs of their skulls, roughly where ours are, but they seem to be

relatively insensitive and I know of no evidence to suggest that they can pick up and interpret, for example, sounds beyond the water. Much more important to them are the vibration-sensitive cells located in their lateral lines – those convenient 'cut here' dotted lines that run down the centre of each side of the body from head to tail. These cells can detect the slightest resonance – footsteps on the bank or on a bridge, or items being dropped or bumped in the bottom of a boat – and serve as an alarm system. They also contain receptors that enable the fish to sense chemicals in the water, including pheromones from other fish.

Taste and smell
That trout have an adequately developed sense of taste and smell is of greater importance to the stillwater flyfisher than to those who fish streams or rivers, but is not vital to either. It seems probable that in lakes and reservoirs, where the fish often have time and opportunity to examine food items at leisure, some smells or flavours may attract them and they may find others repellent. But in streams and rivers, where the food forms (and our artificial flies) are being swept along on the current and where the fish must decide fairly rapidly whether to take an approaching item or not, it seems clear that they rely almost exclusively on their eyesight for the interception of their quarry.

The brown trout's behaviour
Brown trout are intensely territorial. From a very early age, each fish adopts a feeding area as its own and defends it aggressively. The size of the feeding area must be sufficient to provide it with the food it needs and will therefore expand as the trout grows.

Each brown trout generally has two lies – one in its feeding area and the other a bolt hole to which it retreats if danger threatens and in which it rests during non-feeding periods.

The essential requirements of a feeding lie are that it should allow the fish to hang on the current with the least possible expenditure of effort and that it should afford a clear view of food being borne towards it on the stream. Ideally, it will also afford cover in the form of an overhanging bank, bush or tree, or a bridge.

The need for a fish to be able to hang on the current without effort is often met by taking advantage of obstructions. Where the current meets rocks, weed beds, groynes, fallen trees and the like, it slows dramatically, creating a buffer of slow-moving water around which the current flows and thus creating ideal lies for trout, which is why fish are so often found lying immediately upstream of such obstacles. Whorls and eddies can provide the slack water fish need, too, which is why it is not unusual to find fish facing downstream in the slowly rotating water in a small bay, or at the edge of the main current in a mill pool or below a sluice or hatch.

The essential requirement of a bolt hole is that it should provide cover from view and that, again, it should be in slack water. Weed beds and undercut banks are ideal, and it is astonishing how completely a trout can disappear as it slides into some dark recess.

Having found a suitable lie, a brown trout will generally remain on it unless evicted by a more aggressive fish, repeatedly disturbed by anglers or other predators, or unless it spots a more suitable lie to which to decamp. The precision with which a brown trout places itself on its lie, hanging above precisely the same spot on the river bed day after day, even week after week, can be remarkable, and it can be helpful to the flyfisher. The constant tail-waving of a trout lying on one spot, close to the bottom, often sweeps clean a small patch on the river bed, making the fish easier to spot. It is also one of the chief reasons we fish as we do. When a feeding fish has been spotted, we may approach it cautiously, try to identify what it is taking, prepare our tackle and then cast to it, with a reasonable expectation that it will still be lying in the same place, provided we have not been so clumsy as to disturb it.

Also remarkable is the way in which a new fish will move in and take over a lie almost as soon as the original occupant vacates it. Take a trout from an obviously good lie, come back the next day, and the chances are that another fish, often of similar size, will be lying in exactly the same spot.

Capture or disturbance aside, the two things that can be relied upon to induce a brown trout to leave its lie are the mating urge and temporary preoccupation with a particular food form. Trout feeding on shrimps, for example, may wander some distance from their lies, as may those responding to a profusion of nymphs ascending to hatch. When this happens, fish will often be seen lying over submerged weed beds, darting busily from side to side to intercept their prey before it can be swept downstream on the current.

Trout feeding in this way – indeed, trout feeding on anything – tend to be less easily alarmed than non-feeding trout, and the harder they are feeding, the less easily are they alarmed. At one end of the scale, a non-feeding trout, alert but simply hovering on its lie, may be expected to dash for its bolt hole at the slightest movement on its horizon. At the other, a fish hanging just below the surface and rising confidently and regularly every thirty seconds may be almost completely oblivious to an angler on the bank or even, on occasion, to clumsy casting.

One of the most frustrating things about brown trout from the angler's point of view is that much of their feeding is done at night. Visit a prolific fishery very early on a summer morning, just as it is getting light, and the evidence will be plain to see, with empty nymphal shucks and spent spinners drifting on the current and littering the margins, bearing testimony to the recently finished feast. Of course, there are daytime hatches, too; we would have pretty sorry sport if there were not. But it is probable that as much as 70 or 80 per cent of the average brown trout's food is taken during the hours of darkness.

The sea trout's behaviour

It is no coincidence that brown trout that grow up in infertile rivers will be more inclined to migrate to sea than those living in fertile ones – or, put another way, infertile rivers tend to have better sea-trout runs than fertile ones. There is, in fact, a physical trigger for brown-trout migration.

As we have already seen, brown trout are territorial, taking and holding an area sufficiently large to provide them with the food they need. In fertile rivers such as the chalk streams, the area may be quite small, perhaps only a couple of feet wide and three or four feet long, so the river as a whole will have the capacity to sustain large numbers of trout. In infertile rivers, a trout's territory may have to be three or four times as large or more, and the river will be able to support only relatively small numbers of fish.

Where the number of brown trout exceeds a river's capacity to provide food, some of them will be unable to take and hold feeding areas. It is easier to drift down with the current than to swim against it. Therefore, these unsuccessful fish tend to move downstream, eventually reaching estuaries and coastal waters in which they will find an abundance of food. The less adventurous of them will remain in the estuaries as slob trout; the more adventurous will roam further afield as sea trout. Both will return to the rivers of their birth to spawn. There is more than a little irony here. Imagine the chagrin of the brown trout that have remained in the rivers, eking out meagre livings from their hard-won feeding areas, when their less successful brothers and sisters come home – fit, fat and happy, fresh from the sea.

Migrating trout make their way downstream to the estuaries when they are two or three years old, usually between February and April. As they reach brackish water, many of them smolt, turning silver. For reasons we do not understand, some seem already to have decided that they will go no further than the estuary, and they fail to smolt, retaining their brown-trout livery throughout their time in salt or brackish water. Such fish, which may grow to 5 pounds in weight or more, are rather unkindly termed slob trout.

Although their more adventurous relatives leave the estuaries, they seem rarely to go further than they need to in order to find sufficient food. A few tagged fish have been caught considerable distances from home, some from north-east England, for example, having been netted off the Danish coast. But such distant wandering is probably the exception rather than the rule, most sea trout simply cruising up and down the coast, feeding among rocks and beds of seaweed in relatively shallow water.

Many young sea trout remain in saltwater quite briefly, returning to the rivers in which they were born within six to eight months, weighing between ¾ pound and 1½ pounds and being known by an assortment of colloquial names – whitling in Wales and more widely, school peal in Devon, herling and finnock in Scotland. Thereafter, they will return every year until they die. The fishes' life expectancy is variable. About a third of all sea trout survive to make second spawning runs; one in ten spawns for a third time; and only about half of that number achieves a fourth spawning. Thereafter, a tiny and ever-declining number may go on and spawn up to seven or eight times in all. A sea trout returning to freshwater after one winter at sea is likely to weigh between 3 and 5 pounds; after two winters it may weigh between 5 and 10 pounds; and those rare fish that spend three or more winters at sea may grow to 15 or even, very rarely, 20 pounds or more.

While the timing of the runs varies slightly from river system to river system, the best sea-trout fishing is generally to be had in July, August and September, when the peal are running and respectable numbers of larger fish of up to 6 pounds or more are coming through.

On their return to freshwater, sea trout, like salmon, generally stop feeding, living off their body fat until their return to sea after spawning. I say generally because the odd food item may occasionally be found in a sea trout's stomach, and it is not uncommon for peal to be caught on dry flies by anglers fishing for non-migratory brown trout, which suggests that their dormant feeding urge can quite easily be awakened.

People have speculated that this self-starving behaviour serves to conserve the modest food stocks the sea trout's young will need for survival. It seems likely, though, that it may have at least as much to do with habit. By comparison with the sizeable shrimps, small fish and other marine creatures upon which they feed at sea, the food forms available in rivers must seem pretty small, insignificant and unattractive. This may explain, in part at least, why sea trout (and salmon) that do not feed in freshwater will often willingly take fly patterns tied to represent the sorts of creatures they feed on in saltwater but not those designed to represent freshwater invertebrates.

Sea trout can vary considerably in appearance. Some are virtually indistinguishable from non-migratory brown trout, having the same bronze or golden flanks and the same largish, lightly haloed black spots. Others – brilliantly silver and often with neat little black x marks on their flanks – look more like salmon. When they have been in freshwater for a while, even the most glittering of them begin to assume their brown-trout liveries again, and it can become quite difficult to differentiate between a sea trout that has migrated and a non-migratory brown trout of similar size. The only sure way of discovering their respective backgrounds is by putting their scales under a microscope. A fish's scales chart its life history as surely as do a tree trunk's rings, and scales from a migratory fish will show faster growth than those from a non-migratory one.

The most significant characteristic of the sea trout from the angler's point of view – apart, perhaps, from its spectacular fighting ability and its superb culinary qualities – is its shyness. Sea trout are infinitely more easily alarmed than brown trout. Although they can be caught in daylight, especially in streams and rivers in which the water is peat stained, helping to conceal the angler's activities, their wariness generally makes it more profitable to fish for them at night.

The Grayling (*Thymallus thymallus*)

Although quite unlike a trout in appearance and breeding habits, the grayling – the aptly named 'lady of the stream' – wears the salmonid badge in the form of that small, telltale adipose fin on her back between her dorsal fin and her tail, and her diet and behaviour are similar to the trout's.

Grayling are rather more critical of water quality than brown trout, and show a marked preference for cold, very clean, well-oxygenated streams and rivers with plenty of deep, dark pools. Although they may be found in most parts of Great Britain, they do not occur in Ireland. They do best in the chalk streams and in spate rivers in Yorkshire, the north country and Scotland.

The grayling is a handsome fish. With her flat belly and gently arched back, she is beautifully streamlined. Her markings – light grey or bronze on top blending to bright silver flanks lined laterally with black, and a white belly – are much like those of many coarse fish, as are her scales, which are noticeably larger than a trout's. But her single, most obvious distinguishing feature is her dorsal fin, huge, orange, barred and sail-like, which she uses to advantage when hooked – erecting it and paravaning across the current – and which, apparently endearingly but in fact for purely practical reasons, the male folds over his mate's back during spawning. The grayling's eye is interesting, too, with its strangely pear-shaped pupil, which almost certainly serves to enhance her forward binocular vision.

Unlike brown trout, grayling spawn in the spring with the coarse fish and, as a consequence, tend not to regain peak condition until the late summer, being at their best during the autumn and winter. They are prolific creatures, producing vast numbers of young. It is their prolific nature and the fact that their diets are so similar to the trout's that have brought about the disrespect with which some anglers have regarded them and the wars that some keepers have waged on them. But, if their numbers are kept within reasonable bounds, grayling are fine sporting fish. In recent years, flyfishers have come increasingly to recognize this and to value them both in their own right and for the extension to the season they provide.

The grayling is essentially a bottom feeder, as is evidenced by the fact that her mouth is on the small side and low-set, rather than being right at the front of her head as is the trout's. This probably accounts for the way in which she takes an insect from the water's surface, rising from the bottom increasingly steeply until she is almost lying on her back, and then turning sharply downwards having grabbed the fly. This is very different from the trout's gentle upward tilt from a position quite close to the surface, his confident taking of his quarry and his leisurely downward turn.

Grayling do not have the almost unlimited growth potential of trout. A 1 pound grayling is respectable, a 2 pounder is remarkable and the British record is held by a fish of 4 pounds 3 ounces taken from the Dorset Frome in 1989. (In north-west Europe, especially in Austria, Sweden, Finland and Norway, grayling fare noticeably better than they do in Britain, and grow very much larger.)

Grayling generally shoal by year. It is not unusual to find several dozen ½ pound fish sharing a hollow in the river bed or an opening in the weed. Shoals of larger fish will be smaller, and the very largest grayling tend either to be solitary or to be in very small groups.

An unexplained characteristic of grayling, especially large grayling, is their tendency to wander. Where brown trout are concerned, a fish identified one week is likely to be on the same lie the following week and the week after that unless it has been caught or otherwise displaced. The same cannot be said for grayling. Find a couple of large specimens in a clearly identifiable spot, come back a few days later and there is no telling whether they will be there or not. My impression is that the quality of the lie has much to do with this, grayling in really good lies (deep, overhung pools with gentle currents and reliable food supplies) remaining in them for far longer than fish that find themselves in unremarkable ones.

Grayling also differ from trout in their behaviour when alarmed. Although some trout simply sink to the bottom and sulk when danger threatens, most bristle noticeably as they become suspicious and then dart for cover as soon as their fears are confirmed. In contrast, grayling often show very little sign of being aware of danger, but stop feeding and then begin to drift back on the current. When really startled, small ones tend to flee as a shoal, somewhat chaotically.

The Rainbow Trout (*Oncorhynchus mykiss*)

Rainbow trout were first imported into Britain from their native rivers on the western seaboard of the United States during the 1880s. Since then, they have been increasingly widely farmed, both for the table-fish market and for restocking purposes, and they have found their way into a very substantial number of rivers, either by being stocked into them or by escaping from trout farms.

Although rainbow trout can, and do, breed successfully in far more of Britain's rivers than is generally acknowledged, they have been able to generate self-sustaining populations in only very few. It is one thing for fish to deposit ova in the redds and for some of the ova to hatch; it is quite another for the juvenile fish to survive and reach maturity in substantial numbers and to breed successfully. The only British rivers that now appear to support significant, self-regenerating populations of rainbow trout are the Dove and the Wye in Derbyshire, the Missbourne on the Hertfordshire–Buckinghamshire border, the Buckinghamshire Wye, and possibly one or two small Hampshire chalk brooks. There used to be a reasonable head of naturalized rainbow trout in the River Chess in Hertfordshire, but it seems to have died out.

Young rainbow trout, bright silver in colour, can readily be distinguished from salmon and sea-trout smolts and from juvenile brown trout by the dark spots that extend on to their tails and by the relative roundness of the tails themselves. As adults, they are clearly identifiable by the broad, iridescent, pinkish band that runs down their flanks from head to tail and, again, by the fact that they are the only salmonid species to have spots on their tails.

Fast-growing, disease-resistant, tolerant of being crowded together in stew ponds and with a higher temperature-tolerance range than the brown trout, rainbow trout are ideal farm fish, and can provide excellent sport in lakes and reservoirs. In most respects, however, they are less well suited to life in British rivers than the native species.

For reasons that are unclear, rainbow trout stocked into our rivers seem not to thrive as brown trout and grayling do, or as do their siblings stocked into stillwaters. When caught, they tend to be on the lean side and a bit drab; very rarely are they the fit, glittering and brilliantly coloured fish found in their home waters around Mount Shasta or in fertile British reservoirs.

Rainbows are voracious feeders and are inclined to shoal, especially when immature; they therefore compete heavily with brown trout for food and will frequently harass the more sedate browns quite unmercifully. They tend also to be listless, often roaming in search of food. One of the chief pleasures of river fly-fishing is the stalking of individual fish, and it can be very frustrating to spend five or ten minutes on hands and knees, working your way into a position from which you can cast to a particular trout, only to find when you get there that it has wandered off to pastures new. It is for these reasons, as well as for the fact that rainbow trout are so patently alien to Britain, that many people are uncomfortable with their use for stocking British streams and rivers. On the other hand, they do offer the advantages of being relatively inexpensive, of not endangering wild brown trout stocks by cross-breeding and of being easily eradicable. Because they have short life spans (three to five years) and rarely breed successfully in our rivers, any decision to rid a river of rainbows can be promulgated quite quickly simply by ceasing to replenish the stock.

Coarse Fish on Fly

Several species of coarse fish may be taken on fly, pike, perch, chub and dace among them. Pike, which prey on almost all other freshwater species, are very rarely taken on trout or grayling flies, being far more readily tempted by large, fish-like lures stripped past them, or by spoons and spinners. Perch occasionally take deep-fished nymphs, especially those with a bit of gold or bright red in them. Only very rarely, though, can they be tempted with more conventional nymphs, and I do not recall ever having heard of a perch being taken on a dry fly.

Chub and dace are different. Neither of them is a game fish in the accepted sense of that phrase but they are often encountered in trout waters, will take an artificial fly and can provide entertaining sport for flyfishers. They are widely distributed throughout England – although they are absent from Cornwall and rare in the Lake District – and they tend to inhabit the lower, slower-moving stretches of trout streams.

In common with all other coarse fish, chub and dace spawn in late spring or early summer and do not fully recover condition until July or August. Although the young fish are very similar in appearance (they can be told apart by the convex trailing edge to the chub's anal fin as opposed to the dace's concave one), the adults are very different. Chub may grow to 6 pounds or more in weight, and they develop a distinctive bronzy hue; dace rarely reach a pound and remain bright silver.

As adults, the two species behave differently, too. Chub tend to lurk beneath trees and overhanging bushes in small shoals of no more than a dozen or so, and are intensely shy, sinking quietly to the bottom at the first sign of danger. Dace are far more gregarious, often lying in midstream in large shoals, and they seem to be less easily frightened.

It is easy to dismiss chub and dace simply because they are inedible (the poor chub may well be the least edible fish that swims). But they are part of the flyfisher's heritage and are deserving of respect for the sport they may provide on hot and otherwise fishless afternoons, and for the service the dace can perform in honing the flyfisher's reactions in September in preparation for the grayling season to come.

Finally . . . and just for fun, I am assured by Guy Robinson, a hugely experienced and respected keeper on the River Test, that there are carriers and side-streams on the water he manages on which falls of spinners can be so heavy on summer evenings that he has seen the resident eels lying just beneath the surface and rising to spent flies just as trout do.

I am not aware that anyone has ever taken an eel on a dry fly but it would be rather fun to try!

3   The Trout's Food

As we saw in the last chapter, trout and grayling have very catholic tastes, feeding opportunistically on a wide range of creatures. The flies they eat may be divided into two broad categories – aquatic flies and terrestrials. Until quite recently, the former were of greater importance to the fish than the latter, but that has changed on some waters. Especially on the chalk streams of southern England, but on other rivers, too, the years since the Second World War have seen a very serious decline in the numbers of up-winged aquatic flies, and the decline has been become increasingly rapid since the mid 1980s. As a consequence, the relative importance of aquatic and terrestrial insects in the trout's diet has been changing. Possible reasons for the decline are discussed later in this book, but in reading this chapter about the trout's food, and in fishing, it should be born in mind that terrestrial insects – ants, beetles, black gnats, daddy-long-legs, hawthorn flies, reed smuts and the like – have become proportionally more important to the fish than they once were, in some rivers at least.

The aquatic insects trout and grayling eat may be divided into four main groups – up-winged flies, caddis flies, stoneflies and flat-winged flies. A basic understanding of the distribution, appearance and life cycle of each of these groups is important to the angler as, when there is a hatch of flies, it can help us identify what the fish are feeding on and to select an artificial to match it.

Up-Winged Flies (*Ephemeroptera*)

Up-winged flies are found, in greater or lesser numbers, on every stream and river in Great Britain. In their various forms they constitute a substantial part of the trout's food intake and, with the caddis flies, they are the cornerstone upon which river fly-fishing, and especially dry-fly fishing, has traditionally been based.

Some twenty species of up-winged flies are important to fish, and therefore to fishermen, from the tiny Caënis at less than quarter of an inch long to the mayfly, which averages an inch in length, excluding its tails. Their life cycles are all similar, and begin when eggs are laid on the water's surface or, in some species, beneath it.

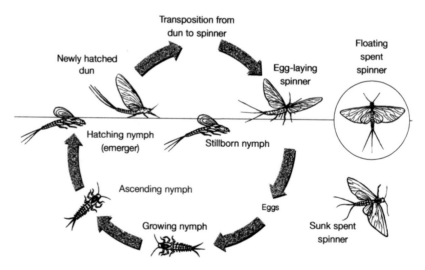

Fig. 3 Up-winged fly's life cycle

The nymphs that hatch from the eggs vary in appearance and habit. Some are relatively flat, which enables them to cling to stones in fast-running water. Others are well camouflaged and slow-moving bottom dwellers. Many are slim and streamlined and can swim rapidly from weed frond to weed frond. One, the mayfly nymph, is strong and bullet-headed, which enables it to burrow into mud and silt on the river bed.

For all their differences, the nymphs of all up-winged flies have many visible characteristics in common. Each has six legs, a small head, a relatively bulbous thorax, which becomes darker and increasingly hump-backed as the nymph matures and its wings develop, a segmented abdomen with gill filaments along either side, and three tails.

As they develop, the nymphs feed busily on decaying vegetable matter – rotting weed, fallen leaves, and so on. Although fish will take growing nymphs when they can, the nymphs themselves are well camouflaged, spend long periods at rest among the weed or in silt or detritus on the river bed, move slowly when they move at all and are therefore difficult to spot.

The nymphs of most up-winged flies mature within six months or a year. The exception is the mayfly, the biggest of them all. This has a variable nymphal period that can last for anything from ten months to two years. It is when they begin their journeys to the surface to hatch that nymphs become particularly vulnerable to predation.

The hatching process is a fascinating one. Before breaking cover, the nymphs of most species build up gaseous layers between their bodies and their outer casings. This probably serves both to increase their buoyancy, helping them in their ascent through the water, and to separate the now fully formed adult fly from its nymphal shuck. When conditions are right, the nymph part-swims and part-floats to the surface, where it hangs in the surface film while the nymphal case splits along its back and the adult fly, the dun, emerges. This can be an astonishingly rapid process, sometimes almost instantaneous, and it needs to be.

During a hatch of flies, trout are constantly on the look-out for hatching insects (emergers) and for stillborn flies – those that fail to struggle clear of their nymphal shucks. However quick the hatching process may be, the emerging adults are trapped, at least momentarily, and they and the stillborn flies offer easy pickings for the fish, as do the newly hatched duns, which remain on the surface of the water only for as long as it takes for their wings to stiffen and dry.

The duns of all up-winged flies are dull, drab, lustreless creatures, with opaque wings and short, often rather limp-looking tails. Their bodies and legs are not greatly dissimilar to those of the nymphs, although the head may be a little larger and the legs are markedly longer. Some species have two large wings, others have a further pair of much smaller ones located behind their main ones and usually overlapping them slightly.

As soon as they are able to, the duns fly up from the water and into trees, bushes or other bankside vegetation, where they remain for anything from twelve to thirty-six hours before rehatching. This is one of the most intriguing and miraculous transformations in nature. Clinging to a leaf or twig, the dun parts its wings and its back splits open, just as the nymph's did, and another fully developed fly, the spinner, emerges complete and perfect in every detail. The spinner is a very much brighter, prettier creature than the dun, with a shiny body, glistening, transparent wings, longer forelegs and either two or three slender tails depending on its species, each as much as twice or three times the insect's body length.

Up-winged spinners usually mate in flight, often repeatedly dancing upwards and drifting down again in the air above the river and the river bank as they do so – a lovely sight against the setting sun on a summer evening. The males die almost as soon as mating has been completed. The females lay their eggs on the water, dipping on to it repeatedly in the process, before dying themselves, floating away spent, spread-eagled on the current. In several species – notably the *Baëtids*, which are the small, medium and large dark olives, the pale watery and the iron blue – the female spinner crawls down a reed stem or the woodwork of a groyne or footbridge to lay her eggs quite deep down in the water.

Spent spinners are warmly welcomed by trout. Whether on the water's surface or beneath it, they represent worthwhile morsels of protein and, as they cannot possibly escape, the fish need expend very little effort in collecting them.

The Caddis Flies or Sedge Flies (*Trichoptera*)

Of the almost 200 species of caddis flies identified in Britain, only about twenty are of any consequence to flyfishers and fewer still are of inter-

A wild brown trout from a Dartmoor stream. Although fish of 1 lb or more are occasionally caught from such waters, fish of ¼ lb to ½ lb are the norm

A fine wild brown trout from the River Tay in Scotland

A stocked brown trout from the River Itchen. Farm-reared they may be, but such fish can quickly become both fussy and shy

In her element: a brown trout on her lie in a chalk stream

A fine 4 lb sea trout – the shyest of all game fish

The grayling – the 'lady of the stream' and a fine game fish in her own right

Rainbow trout are not native to Britain and spawn successfully in very few British rivers, but a number of fishery managers stock their rivers with them

Releasing a wild brown trout on the River Piddle in Dorset. Fish being returned should be held gently, facing into the current, until they swim away

Waiting and watching: the successful river fly fisher spends at least as much time watching the water as actually fishing

Early season on the Itchen. John Fairrie fishing at Abbotts Barton

John Goddard playing a fish on Highland Burn at Abbotts Barton on the River Itchen. For students of angling history, this is precisely the place at which G.E.M. Skues suddenly 'discovered' nymph fishing

Striking is a misnomer: simply tighten into the fish as if lifting into a back-cast

A summer idyll. The author fishing on the River Frome in Dorset

Tightening into a fish on the River Piddle in Dorset

The author playing a fish on the River Piddle in Dorset

est on streams and rivers. Nevertheless, those few are of considerable importance.

Female caddis flies lay their eggs on the water's surface or by crawling beneath it, very much as the up-winged flies do, and the eggs sink to the river bed or adhere to weed where they eventually hatch as larvae. Caddis larvae vary from a quarter of an inch to an inch in length. Ponderous and juicy, they are extremely vulnerable to predation by trout and other fish, and most of them protect themselves by building cases around their grub-like bodies. The cases are constructed from a wide variety of bits and pieces – mud, grains of sand, discarded tiny snail shells, bits of twig and reed stem cut to length. Each species is particular about the material it uses and the method of construction, and the case serves both to camouflage the larva and to protect it physically from predators. With their bodies safely encased and just their heads and legs sticking out, the larvae lumber about the river bed feeding on decaying vegetation and, occasionally, other smaller insects.

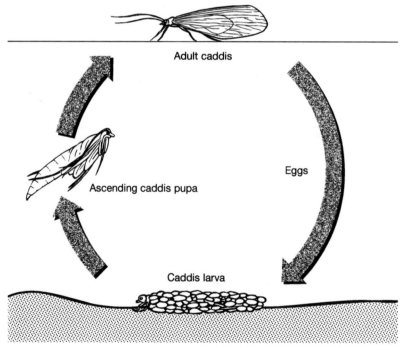

Adult caddis

Ascending caddis pupa

Eggs

Caddis larva

Fig. 4 Caddis life cycle

At its appointed time, usually after about a year, the larva retreats into its case, eventually to emerge as a pupa. The pupal phase in the insect's life is relatively brief, serving only to facilitate transition from the river bed to the water's surface, where the adult fly hatches. The pupae of some caddis species climb clear of the water to hatch, while others simply hatch in the surface film where the adults' desperate, scuttling efforts to get airborne make them attractive targets for trout.

At rest, adult caddis are not unlike moths in general appearance, folding their four wings into neat roof shapes over their backs. But their wings are, in fact, covered with very fine hairs, while a moth's are scaled, and caddis flies generally have distinctively long antennae.

Adult caddis flies mate on shore and among the waterside vegetation rather than in flight, the females returning to the water to lay their eggs and, again, to become vulnerable to predation by fish.

Although trout eat caddis larvae and pupae, river flyfishers generally concentrate their attentions on the winged adults for both practical and traditional reasons. The practical basis for this is the difficulty of fishing an artificial caddis larva realistically slowly on the river or stream bed where the naturals live. The traditional one probably has to do with reservations about fishing necessarily heavily weighted nymphs to trout in streams and rivers.

The Stoneflies (*Plecoptera*)

The stoneflies, of which there are some thirty species in Britain, are found in and on the banks of stony rivers, chiefly in Scotland, Ireland and the north of England. Where they occur elsewhere, they generally do so in numbers too small to be of any real interest to fish or fishermen. The exception, perhaps, is the willow fly, which may be seen on and around gravel-bedded rivers throughout the United Kingdom in August and September.

Stoneflies have three-phase life cycles. The nymphs hatch from eggs stuck to stones and rocks on the river bed and live on the bottom, moulting as many as thirty times before eventually clambering ashore to hatch. They are strong crawlers and are readily distinguishable from the nymphs of up-winged flies by the fact that they have only two, quite short, jointed tails, and by their two relatively long antennae. They range from a quarter of an inch to just over an inch in length and, while the smaller species feed on algae and organic debris, the larger ones are fearsome predators, preying on up-winged flies' nymphs, midge larvae and caddis fly larvae, and even on the nymphs of other stoneflies.

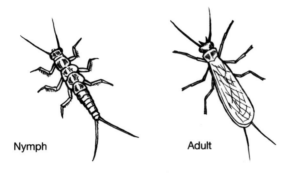

Nymph   Adult

Fig. 5 Stoneflies

The nymphal, or creeper, stage of the stonefly's life lasts for between one and three years, depending upon the species. At the end of this time, it crawls ashore for its final moult, which produces the winged adult.

Like the nymphs, the adults each have two antennae and two tails. Their wings, set in two pairs, are hard and glossy, and are laid curved over their backs in a somewhat shell-like configuration when the insects are at rest. The female is generally the better flyer, if still a little clumsy, and, in some species, the male's wings are almost vestigial, covering no more than half the length of the insect's body and being effectively useless.

Adult stoneflies are essentially land-based creatures. They scuttle around among the rocks and boulders on the river bank, rarely moving far from the water, and they mate on land. Having done so, the female flies back to the water where she deposits her eggs – some species walk across the surface depositing small clumps of ova as they go, others dip repeatedly on to the water, and one or two simply crash land, releasing all their eggs at once as they do so.

Trout and particularly grayling feed on stonefly nymphs, nosing around among the pebbles on the bottom in search of them, and they also take the egg-laying females enthusiastically.

The Flat-Winged Flies (*Diptera*)

The order Diptera is one of the largest in the insect world, including all the houseflies, midges, mosquitoes, daddy-long-legs, and so on. Surprisingly few of its members are of interest to fish or flyfishers and, of those that are, the majority are of far greater importance on stillwaters than on streams and rivers. However, midges seem largely to have been unaffected by the environmental changes that have brought about the decline in the numbers of up-winged flies. Artificials, especially those designed to represent their pupae, can be useful additions to the river flyfisher's armoury.

Midges have four-stage life cycles. Female midges lay their eggs in gelatinous clumps either on the water's surface or on weed fronds. The larvae that eventually hatch vary enormously in size (from an eighth of an inch to over an inch) and colour, from grey through assorted shades of green and brown to red, the red ones generally predominating and giving rise to the 'bloodworm' appellation, widely used by anglers. All of them are slender and worm-like in appearance and most propel themselves with a peculiar, figure-of-eight lashing movement. Having hatched, they sink to the river bed, where they live among the decaying vegetation upon which they feed. Midge larvae are difficult for the river flyfisher to represent with artificials, but some of the bloodworm patterns devised for stillwaters can be effective on rivers.

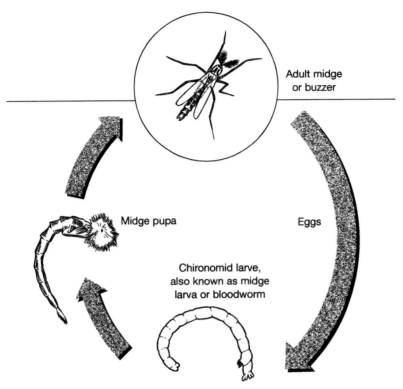

Fig. 6 The chironomid, 'midge' or 'buzzer' life cycle

At their appointed times, usually about a year after hatching and having undergone several moults, the larvae pupate, the emergent pupae being distinctively comma-shaped. Each one has a somewhat bulbous thorax, from which protrudes a tuft of breathing filaments, and a slender, curved, usually clearly segmented abdomen tipped with a tiny bunch of gill fibres. When they are ready to hatch, the pupae, quite competent swimmers, make their way to the top of the water. There they lie horizontally suspended under the surface film before splitting to release the adult midge. In some species, the hatching process is very quick; in others, or on warm still evenings when the surface film of the water is dense, it may take some time for the winged adults to break through. The semi-trapped hatching adults are taken enthusiastically by trout and grayling. Once hatched, adult midges almost always fly off at once, minimizing the period of time during which they are most vulnerable.

There is clearly room for a great deal more experimentation than has yet been done with small midge pupa patterns – probably in sizes 12 to 16 – fished as nymphs on streams and rivers, just beneath the surface film, and with 'damp' imitations of the spent adult.

Adult midges mate in flight, often forming tall, smoky columns in the lee of trees, hedgerows and buildings on warm evenings. The females then return to the water to lay their eggs.

The Alder (*Sialis lutaria*)

Alder flies, an inch long, dark-brown, caddis-like, appear in large numbers throughout Britain in May, and although artificials, both wet and dry, dressed to represent them can be very effective, I know of no evidence to suggest that trout actually feed on the naturals. Some people swear by them, but there does not seem to be much rationale for their use. I shall not therefore describe the fly's life cycle or behaviour, but instead simply note that the artificials can sometimes be useful general patterns.

The Freshwater Shrimp (*Gammarus pulex*)

Freshwater shrimps are found in all clean, alkaline streams and rivers in Britain, often in prodigious numbers. Averaging about half an inch in length, they curl themselves up when at rest and straighten out as they start to swim. Seeking shelter in the weed and among the pebbles on the stream bed, they are a dull, light yellow-ochre colour for most of the year, turning a much deeper orange-yellow as the mating season approaches in spring or early summer.

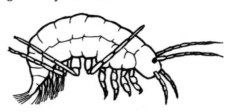

Fig. 7 Freshwater shrimp

Trout and grayling feed on shrimps enthusiastically, foraging around among the weed roots for them, sometimes in shallow streams, with their tails waving in the air in a rather silly way. The fish may be taken on any of the several artificials designed to represent the shrimp or on Frank Sawyer's Killer Bug, a patently shrimp-like pattern.

Heavily weighted shrimp patterns can be useful for winkling trout out of unusually deep, difficult lies. Speaking purely personally, though, and while I have no reservations whatever about using leaded dressings on stillwaters, I am inclined to reserve them on rivers for otherwise wholly inaccessible fish rather than resort to them as regular panaceas when there are almost always more delicate and subtle options available.

Terrestrial Insects

As we saw earlier, the recent decline in up-winged fly hatches on the chalk streams and elsewhere has made trout increasingly dependent upon terrestrial insects for surface food. The following list of the main terrestrial food forms, with descriptions of their appearances, seasons and suggested artificials, should enable the reader to anticipate the most important of the myriad species born on land, and to make the most of them when they occur.

Ants (*Hymenoptera*)

Surefooted, ants rarely fall on to the water from bankside vegetation or overhanging branches, and are therefore surprisingly rarely available to trout in the normal course of events. But, from time to time, usually on heavy, humid, thundery days in mid- to late summer, they develop wings and take to the air. When this happens, they are sometimes blown on to the water in great numbers, and the fish take full advantage of this manna from heaven. Flights of ants always seem to last for less than a week, and falls of them on streams and rivers rarely continue for more than a couple of hours or so, but the angler with a few appropriate artificials in his fly box can have a field day during that time.

Beetles (*Coleoptera*)

Unlike ants, all shapes, sizes and colours of beetles come to grief on the water, and they appear at all stages of the season. They can make a significant contribution to the diet of trout in small, heather-girt and otherwise relatively barren upland streams, and in streams and rivers heavily overhung with trees and bushes.

Although some species – most notably the soldier and sailor beetles and the Coch-y-bonddu – are well known to anglers, being blown on to the water in large numbers (usually in midsummer), there are in fact so many different species that may become available to the trout that it is probably best simply to rely on one or two general patterns with which to represent them all. While some modern artificials have been devised specifically to imitate particular beetles, my own experience suggests that they appeal more to fishermen than fish, the latter preferring more general dressings.

Black Gnats and Reed Smuts (*Bibio spp and Simulium spp*)

Black gnat is a generic term used by flyfishers to encompass several small (quarter of an inch long), black, flat-winged terrestrial fly species that may be blown on to streams and rivers at almost any stage in the season, from May until September. Black gnats are always warmly welcomed by trout and, as falls of them are so common, they are of considerable importance to flyfishers.

Reed smuts are similar to black gnats in appearance, but very much smaller. Trout often feed on them greedily and can sometimes become wholly preoccupied with them. Their minuteness makes them difficult to represent on a hook, but a simple blob of black seal's fur dubbing wound on to a tiny hook – size 20 or 22 – will sometimes do the trick.

The Crane Flies (*Tipula spp*)

The crane fly or daddy-long-legs is another terrestrial flat-winged fly that is quite often blown on to the water, especially in grassland areas,

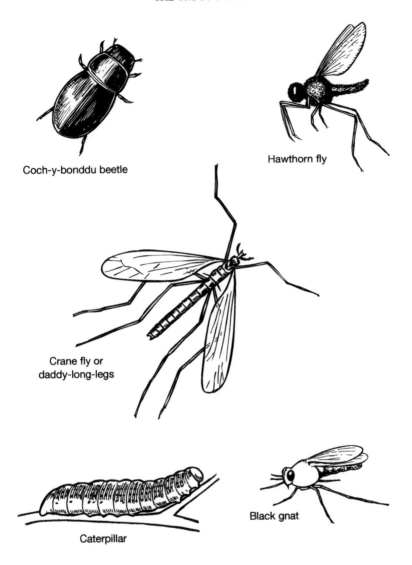

Coch-y-bonddu beetle

Hawthorn fly

Crane fly or
daddy-long-legs

Caterpillar

Black gnat

Fig. 8 Terrestrial insects

to the benefit of the trout and, potentially, of the angler. Indeed, on some chalk-stream fisheries, where hatches of up-winged flies have become scarce, the artificial Daddy now accounts for more fish than almost any other pattern. Gone are the days when it was useful to have a few tucked away in the corner of the fly box; for many people they have become the dry fly of choice from the middle of the season onwards, when the naturals are about.

There are some 300 species of crane flies native to Britain, ranging in size from several that, at a quarter of an inch long, are no larger than black gnats to the grand-daddy of them all, *Tipula maxima*, with a body length of almost one and a half inches. Crane flies are familiar to almost everyone and are instantly recognizable by their extraordinarily long gangling legs and their quite remarkable lack of control in the air. When they fly or are blown out over the water, they frequently stumble across the surface and eventually collapse into it, where the fish take them enthusiastically.

There are several good crane fly patterns, most of them looking extremely realistic even to the human eye. The most important consideration when selecting an artificial is that it should float well, not perched up high like an up-winged dun pattern, but with its body flush with the water's surface.

The Hawthorn Fly (*Bibio marci*)

The hawthorn fly is one of nature's great gifts to trout and to trout fishers early in the season. About half an inch long, with a furry, jet-black body, translucent grey wings and two distinctive long, trailing black legs, it appears towards the end of April, remains with us until about mid May and is often blown on to the water in considerable numbers. When it is, the fish take it unhesitatingly and seem to be almost as uncritical of an artificial as they are of the natural.

It is said that the natural sinks when it arrives on the water. Although I have had many excellent days fishing during falls of hawthorn flies, I have not been able fully to confirm this, but it is certainly true that a 'damp' pattern fished in or just below the surface film often seems to be at least as effective as a high-floating dry one.

Moths (*Lepidoptera*)

Although they fall or are blown on to the water individually and occasionally, generally during the evening, moths are often taken greedily by trout, possibly because of their size and evident helplessness, and an artificial can sometimes deceive even the most difficult fish, particularly late in the evening.

Choice of pattern does not seem to be too critical – almost any cream or brown one may be tied on with reasonable confidence. Personally, I have had some considerable success – and one of my biggest ever brown trout from a river – with a bushy, white pattern tied with a soft, floppy, cree hackle.

4 Tackling Up

One of the great pleasures of river fly-fishing is that it requires very little tackle – a rod, a reel, a line, a leader and a few flies are all you really need. Most of us would wish to add a spool of tippet material and a pair of snippers, some fly floatant, a small tub of Mucilin and, perhaps, a landing net and a priest. Unlike coarse angling and, to a lesser extent, stillwater trouting, river fly-fishing is a mobile pursuit, and it pays to embark upon it lightly laden, keeping tackle as near this necessary minimum as possible.

Wear a fishing waistcoat by all means (I do), or a belt packer; it will enable you to carry everything you need neatly stored and ready to hand, but resist the urge to find something to put in every single pocket. Creels, fishing bags, picnic baskets and suitcases full of flies should be banished from the riverside altogether.

None of this is to say that we should not take with us what we need, or that we can get away with ill-chosen or ill-matched tackle. Good, well-balanced equipment is essential both to confidence and to consistent success (the two go hand in hand), and two of the great benefits of river fly-fishing are that we need relatively little tackle and that even the very best is not outrageously expensive.

It might seem logical to choose a rod first and then to match the fly-line or lines to it. In fact, it is not. The weight and profile of the line to be used is dictated by the size and nature of the water we mean to fish, and the line should therefore be chosen first, a suitable rod then being matched to it.

Fly-lines

Fly-lines, generally consisting of a braided dacron core covered with a plastic coating, provide the weight that is used to work the fly rod when casting and to roll the line out over the water, presenting the fly (we hope) delicately and accurately. They come in a burgeoning and bewildering array of profiles, weights, densities and colours. The first three of these factors are reduced to an Association of Fishing Tackle Manufacturers' (AFTM) code, printed on the box – DT5F, for example; the fourth is self-evident.

The first letter or letters of the code indicate whether a line is double-tapered (DT), weight-forward (WF) or a shooting head or shooting taper (ST). The number represents the weight in drams of the first 10 yards of the line, excluding the 2 feet of level line at the end. And the last letter or letters show whether the line is a floater (F), a sinker (S), a sink-tip (F/S) or an intermediate (I). So our DT5F is a double-tapered floating line, the first 10 yards of which weigh five drams. Similarly, a WF7F/S would be a weight-forward line, the first 10 yards weighing seven drams, the front section sinking and the remainder floating.

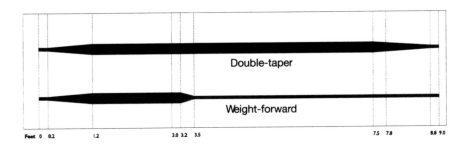

Fig. 9 Fly line profiles

A double-tapered line is level for 2 feet at each end, then tapers over 10 feet to a markedly heavier centre section 22 yards long. It is relatively easy to cast with, turns over neatly, can be made to land lightly on the water and has the added advantage of being reversible. That is to say, when one end becomes worn the line can be reversed on the reel, extending its life probably by a further season or two. The reversibility of a double-tapered line does not double its life as some manufacturers would have you believe. From the moment it is taken from its wrapping, a fly-line starts to dry out, the plasticizer that provides its suppleness evaporating. By the time it has been in use for two or three seasons, the back half will have lost almost as much plasticizer as the front half and will be becoming prone to wear and cracking. The tubs of replasticizer available from some tackle shops will rejuvenate a line temporarily but can only extend its life for a season or so.

Weight-forward lines are level for their first 2 feet, then taper up over 10 feet to a substantially heavier 10 yard belly, tapering down again quite steeply to some 18 yards of fine, level, running line. They are a little less easy to cast with than double-tapers – and rapidly go out of control if the belly is extended beyond the rod tip during casting – and they tend to land on the water rather less delicately than a double-taper does. But they do enable the angler to cast further than he could with a double-taper. Weight-forward lines are chiefly of use on stillwaters, where distance casting is often called for, but there may be a place for one in the armoury of the flyfisher who regularly fishes large rivers.

In profile, a shooting head is essentially the front third to a half of a double-tapered line spliced at its thickest point to a fine running line, usually of braided nylon or flattened nylon monofilament. Although some stillwater anglers can cast prodigious distances with shooting heads, the backing line tends to be prone to tangling and to be uncomfortable to handle, and there is little to be said for the use of shooting heads on streams or rivers.

There has been a fad recently for using very light lines, in the weight range #1 to #3 – and a fad it is. Such lines may be fun to play with in still conditions, but they are very difficult to control in all but the lightest of breezes, even in the most expert hands. At the other end of the scale, lines rated #9 and over are too heavy and indelicate for trout and grayling fishing on streams and rivers. So, for most of our purposes, we should consider lines in the range #4 to #8. In fact, #4s, still on the light side, are probably best reserved for small streams and brooks, and for very clear chalk streams where accuracy and delicacy are at a premium and where distance casting is almost never required. Lines rated #7 or #8 can be useful for sea trout fishing on large rivers or where strong winds may be expected – in Patagonia or the Falkland Islands, as examples. But, lines rated #5 or #6 will generally be ideal for most river fly-fishing.

Floating lines are by far the most widely used for fly-fishing on streams and rivers. Rarely is the water deep enough to justify the use of a sinking line or a sink-tip. A floating line can be lifted from the water and recast quickly, whereas a sinker or sink-tip must either be retrieved and recast, or the angler must do a roll cast to bring the line to the surface before recasting. Floating lines are far less likely to snag on weed beds and other underwater obstructions than are sinkers or sink-tips.

Nevertheless, even though they are less easy to cast with than floating lines because they are made up from two lines of different densities, there may be a place for a sink-tip on a large river, especially when fishing for sea trout or grayling lying well down in deep pools. A medium sinker (Wet Cell 2 or equivalent) may be useful for sea-trout fishing where it is necessary to get the fly down several feet in fast-flowing water. It is true, also, that sinking lines create far less surface disturbance than floating ones and that they are therefore far less obvious to the fish. This can make a case for using an intermediate, with its almost neutral buoyancy, when fishing wet flies in clear water on calm days, especially for sea trout, which can be extremely shy.

Over the years, there has been much inconclusive debate about the most suitable colours for fly-lines. For apparently obvious reasons, people have argued for sky blue or heron grey ones. The fact is, though, that any fly-line in the air or lying on the water must appear to the fish as a virtually black silhouette, whatever its hue. It therefore matters not that manufacturers make lines available in an assortment of colours. Floating lines tend to be pale – pale blue, ivory, peach or even white – and sinking ones are generally made in darker shades of brown or green, or are transparent.

Far more important than its colour is a fly-line's reflective qualities, the extent to which it glints or shines. There is incontrovertible evidence to show that the flash from a line in the air is startlingly evident from the trout's viewpoint and must be one of the commonest causes of alarm in our quarry. Those who doubt this should study the remarkable photographs in Brian Clarke and John Goddard's excellent book, *The Trout and the Fly*. One manufacturer has recently begun production of a good-quality, drab-coloured, matt-surfaced floating line, which seems very promising. The sooner his competitors follow suit the better.

And speaking of quality, there can be no doubt that where fly-lines are concerned, you get what you pay for. The prices asked for what may appear to be no more than lengths of plastic-coated string may seem high, but there is a world of difference between the cheapest and the most expensive, and it really does pay to buy the best line or lines you can afford.

Fly Rods

Although some people still cling to cane rods for sentimental reasons or from a sense of tradition, the vast majority of modern fly rods are made from carbon fibre or a composite of carbon fibre and fibreglass.

Cane rods are built from carefully cut and bonded triangular sections of male Tonkin bamboo. They still have a large following, especially among experienced and traditionally minded river flyfishers. Length for length they are heavier than their carbon fibre and composite counterparts, but they often have gentle actions and can deliver a fly accurately and delicately. They are expensive, though, and, sentiment apart, offer little real advantage over carbon fibre.

Carbon-fibre rods are built by wrapping carbon-fibre tape impregnated with epoxy resin round a mandrel, applying heat to harden the resin and then removing the mandrel. As a material, carbon fibre is expensive, so fibreglass is usually combined with it for the manufacture of inexpensive rods.

Carbon fibre has three major qualities. It is light, which makes for effortless casting over long periods; it is strong and rods made from it are therefore slender and cut through the wind efficiently; and the tip of a well-designed carbon rod stops dead at the end of a forward cast instead of bouncing up and down, enabling the competent angler to put out a straighter line than he might otherwise be able to.

Two warnings should be issued in relation to carbon fibre and composite rods.

First, carbon-fibre rods of whatever quality are by no means indestructible. Working them with insufficient line extended can set up stresses leading to instantaneous breakage, usually 6 or 8 inches above the handle, and a nick caused by a fly striking the rod during casting can cause similar weakness, the fracture often occurring without warning weeks or months later, typically 6 to 8 inches below the tip.

Second, many inexpensive rods advertised as being made of carbon fibre are, in fact, made of composite material. In order to keep costs down, the manufacturers of some blanks have reduced the actual carbon content significantly but continue to make very light and slender rods with the debased material. The resultant rods tend to be both limper in action and markedly more fractile than those with a higher carbon content. It is almost always a false economy to buy a very cheap carbon-fibre rod.

Regardless of what a rod is made of, three other factors should influence the choice – line rating, length and action.

Line rating

Nowadays, every good fly rod is marked just above the handle with the weight of line or the range of line weights to which it is best suited, for example #5 or #4-6. This rating assumes that 10 yards of line will be aerialized. For every 2 yards more or less aerialized in actual fishing, the line needs to be one size lighter or heavier to load the rod correctly. So if you usually fish a small brook on which you rarely expect to cast further than about 8 yards, you may find it helpful to overload your rod by one number – for example, by using a #5 line on a #4 rod.

Beware of rods rated for a wide range of line weights. Whatever a manufacturer may claim, every rod must have a line weight to which it is best suited, and to move away from this optimum must inevitably inhibit the rod's performance. Personally, I tend to be wary of any rod marked with anything more than two, adjacent, AFTM numbers – for example, #4-5.

Length

Perhaps slightly surprisingly, the lengths of rods used for stream and river fishing vary more than do those of rods used on stillwaters. For most purposes, on the chalk streams and on medium-sized spate rivers, an 8½ foot or a 9 foot rod will serve very well. But on small becks and brooks, heavily overhung with trees and bushes, it may be necessary to go down to 7½ or even 7 feet in order to be able to work a line out without constantly catching leaves and branches. On large rivers, a 10 foot rod may be needed to cover the water and to keep in touch with the flies, especially when fishing a wet fly or a team of wet flies upstream.

On the whole, it is sensible to buy a slightly longer rod than you think you need, rather than a shorter one. Although 7 foot and 7½ foot wands are very pretty, they can pose quite serious problems when fishing from the bank; they make it difficult to cast and to retrieve line over reeds, rushes and nettles, to control the line on the water, and to play fish, especially in heavily weeded waters. Unless you habitually wade beneath a canopy of foliage, an 8½ foot or even a 9 foot rod should not prove too long for even the smallest stream, and it should be long enough to cope with all but the largest rivers.

Action

Any fly rod's action is described in terms of the part of its length over which it bends most freely, and of its overall stiffness or flexibility.

A rod that is stiff throughout most of its length and only starts to flex easily towards its tip is said to be tip-actioned, and one that flexes progressively from butt to tip is said to have an all-through action. Regardless of whereabouts a rod flexes along its length, the amount that it will bend under a given load is described in terms of stiffness or softness.

A tip-actioned rod demands a fairly brisk casting action and the loop of the line as it turns over at the ends of the forward and back casts tends to be fairly narrow, which makes for good casting into a wind. The nearer the action gets to the butt, the slower the casting action and the wider the loop. A slow-actioned rod will present a fly more delicately than a fast- or tip-actioned one, but will be less effective in cutting through a breeze. Most river flyfishers find that a moderately stiff all-through action will meet most of their needs.

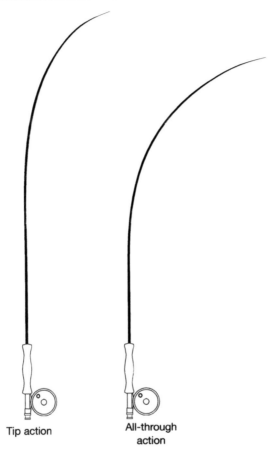

Tip action   All-through action

Fig. 10 Rod actions

Until quite recently, the ferrules used to join one section of a rod to the next interfered with the rod's action, and we were generally advised therefore to choose a rod with the least possible number of sections. The spigot ferrules used on modern carbon-fibre rods have changed all that, having no noticeable effect on the rod's action. It is therefore entirely practicable nowadays to produce truly excellent rods with four, five or even six pieces. Although two- or three-piece rods may be more convenient in some ways, multi-piece ones can be very useful when travelling and, at least as important, make it easy to conceal expensive rods in car boots to avoid attracting thieves.

A brief description of the three rods I use for river fly-fishing, carefully chosen and the product of many years' trial and occasional error, may be of help although I do not pretend that they would suit every angler or every fishing situation.

The first is a beautiful, 7 foot cane brook rod, rated #4, which is remarkably accurate given its quite slow action. It is used less than either of the others but comes into its own on heavily overgrown streams in Devon and Hampshire where I like to wade up through arcades of trees, casting in beneath the banks and to gaps among the tree roots for trout that, I fondly imagine, go largely unharried for the rest of the year.

The second is a four-piece, 8½ foot, #5-rated carbon-fibre model that I have had for ten years now. Its crisp, tip-action enables it to throw a very tight loop, providing accuracy and delicacy even into quite a stiff breeze. It is the most heavily used of the three. It is ideal for use on the chalk streams of southern England, on which I am fortunate to be able to do much of my fishing, and has served similarly well on waters as diverse as the upper Bann in Northern Ireland, the Usk in Wales, the Eden and the Eamont in Cumbria, and, further afield, on the Battenkill in Vermont and the Yellowstone, the Lamar and the Snake rivers in the Rockies.

The third is a 10 foot, #7 carbon-fibre rod which I bought primarily for stillwater fishing. With a fairly stiff tip action, I use it from the bank and from boats on lakes and reservoirs, large and small, and it is the mainstay of my stillwater armoury. But it serves also as my primary sea-trout rod, both in Britain and in the Falkland Islands, where the sea trout grow very fit and fierce and can test a rod to its limits. It is a delight to use, will comfortably cast 25 yards of double-tapered #7 line accurately and without effort, and can stop even the most ferocious sea trout in its tracks when called upon to do so.

Fly Reels

A fly reel is a necessary encumbrance, a receptacle for line that is not in use. The flyfisher does not cast from a fly reel as the coarse or sea angler does from a centre-pin, a fixed-spool or a multiplying reel; nor does he use the reel to retrieve his flies as he would were he spinning; nor is it strictly necessary to use the reel when playing a fish although we shall discuss the pros and cons of doing so in due course.

Much nonsense used to be written about the way in which a reel should balance a rod, bringing the rod's centre of gravity back towards the angler's hand. The assumption was that this was beneficial but it is, in truth, pure baloney. If you disbelieve me, work out 15 yards or so of line, remove the reel from the rod and then carry on casting – you will find the rod noticeably more comfortable to handle without the reel than with it.

The chief requirements of a fly reel are that it should be light and reliable and that it should be just large enough to accommodate the fly-line and a reasonable amount of backing.

Personally, I dislike multiplying and automatic reels, both of which seem to me to be unnecessarily heavy and too prone to mechanical failure. All of my reels are perfectly straightforward, single-action models, with disc drags, exposed rims – which facilitate the control of occasional maverick fish – and plenty of holes cut into the faces of the spools to allow the line and backing to dry reasonably quickly and to help reduce the overall weights of the reels.

The one really significant development in reel design in recent years has been the introduction of large arbor models. As in most things, they have their advantages and disadvantages. On the one hand, the larger circumference of the arbor – the spindle around which the line and backing are wound – undoubtedly reduces the extent to which the line develops memory coils – those nasty, stiff, twists that affect every fly-line or length of nylon when it has been wrapped tightly around a spool for a while. It also enables a significantly faster retrieve without resort to infamously fallible gearing systems. On the other hand, large arbor reels are rather bulkier than traditional ones, sometimes to the point of being burdensome, especially in the larger sizes. Which one chooses is really a matter of personal preference.

Backing Line

Backing line is almost as essential as the fly-line itself. Especially in river fly-fishing, it is very rare for some leviathan to charge off towards the horizon, tearing off the whole of a fly-line and much backing besides. I can recall no more than half a dozen occasions in almost fifty years of fly-fishing when I have been taken down to the backing by trout. Two or three of them involved sea trout in estuaries and the others, all on reservoirs, all involved foul-hooked fish. Day by day, the backing line's primary and essential purpose is to pad out the hard spindle of the reel, reducing the extent to which the fly-line develops memory coils.

Backing line should be waterproof, both to prevent it from swelling when wet and from rotting. Braided, 20 pounds breaking strain dacron or polyester is ideal. Between them, the backing and the fly-line should fill the drum of the reel to within about a quarter of an inch of its rim.

Leaders

The leader – the length of nylon that connects the fly to the fly-line is one of the most vital items of the flyfisher's tackle and one of the most often neglected. It must be so designed as to transmit power evenly from the fly-line, rolling out neatly and delicately over the water, long enough to distance the fly from the potentially fish-frightening fly-line, fine enough to go unnoticed by the trout and strong enough to withstand a fierce take or a charging run from an unexpectedly large fish. From all this, it must be evident that a single length of 4, 6, or 8 pound nylon will not suffice.

The ideal length for a leader for stream and river fly-fishing is between 9 and 12 feet. On small burns and brooks it may be necessary to reduce this to as little as 7 feet because of the short distances being cast and the limited space available.

In order to transmit power from the fly-line smoothly and efficiently right down to the fly, the butt end of the leader should be as nearly the same thickness as the fly-line as possible, certainly no less than half the fly-line's diameter, and the taper should become progressively steeper towards the point.

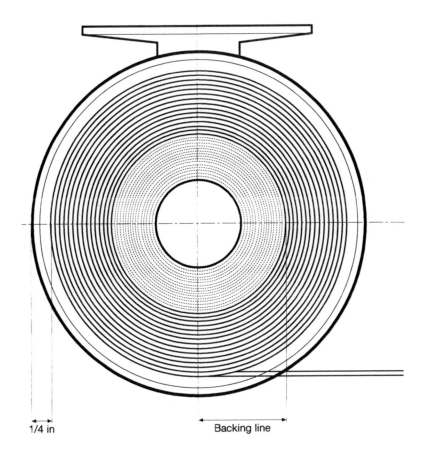

1/4 in   Backing line

Fig. 11 Correct loading of a fly reel

In days gone by, we used a variety of more or less reliable knots to attach leaders to fly-lines. The chief problem they posed was that they were all lumpy and that none of them would run smoothly through the rod rings. All that changed with the introduction of braided loops in the mid 1980s. A braided loop – about 6 inches of hollow braided nylon with a loop at the end – is by far the simplest, neatest and most certain means of securing the leader to the fly-line. The braid is simply slipped over the tip of the fly-line and a short rubberized sleeve is then run back up the braid to cover its back end to prevent it from fraying. It is worth seeping a drop of superglue in beneath the sleeve to secure it. It is also important to check the fly-line immediately behind the sleeve regularly. It is at this point that the line flexes frequently and quite sharply, its coating eventually beginning to crack. When this happens, the fly-line should be cut just behind the damaged area and a new braided loop attached.

If braided loops have changed our lives for the better, the same cannot be said of so-called braided leaders. A braided leader consists simply of between 5 and 9 feet of tapered, braided material to which a tippet of level monofilament is attached. Seen against the light, it is no less visible or intrusive than the fly-line of which it is an extension, which seems to me wholly to defeat the object of the exercise – to distance the fly from the fly-line. At risk of incurring the wrath of the tackle trade, I feel bound to say that they are really little more than an ingenious means of extracting money from innocent anglers' pockets. A straightforward, tapered nylon monofilament leader is a far better option.

There was a time when we made up our own leaders to complicated formulae, using lengths of nylon monofilament of various breaking strains. Knots greatly reduce the breaking strain of nylon – some say by up to 50 per cent – so such leaders were less than entirely reliable, and the knots themselves tended to pick up scum and algae from the water, making them increasingly visible.

Nowadays, commercially made, knotless, tapered leaders, available from tackle dealers, offer a far better alternative. Loop-to-loop connections tend to be a bit bulky, so I generally cut off the loop from the leader and attach its butt end directly to the braided loop using a tucked half-blood knot. Then, using a three-turn water knot, I add 12 to 18 inches of level monofilament to the front end as a tippet. Changing flies inevitably shortens the tippet and I replace it when it gets down to about 8 inches.

A number of new tippet materials have come on to the market in recent years. Described variously as double-strength, fluorocarbon and copolymer, they all claim to offer advantages over regular nylon monofilament, including being finer, breaking strain for breaking strain. I have tried most of them and find myself unmoved. They all seem to lack the slight stretchiness of conventional nylon, which helps

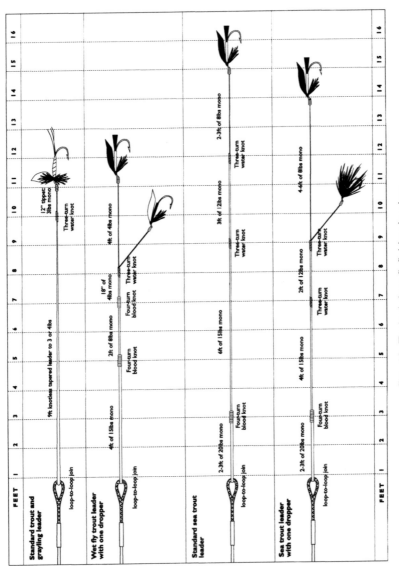

Fig. 12 Typical river flyfishing leaders

cushion the leader against fierce takes or over-enthusiastic striking. They all have a tendency to curl up into ugly and irremovable pig-tails when abraded against anything; and I have been unable to satisfy myself that knots tied with them, however carefully, are as reliable as knots tied in conventional nylon. I believe, too, that the differences in diameters between hi-tech monofilaments and nylon are so marginal as to be inconsequential. For all these reasons, I find myself still using a traditional, conventional nylon monofilament, and would only be happier with it if it had a matt finish rather than a gloss one, which I have to remove with a mixture of fuller's earth, glycerine and detergent.

Generally speaking, point strengths of leaders for river fly-fishing are lighter than those used in stillwater trouting, partly because trout in running water are often smaller and tend neither to take so fiercely nor to run so far as those in lochs, lakes and reservoirs, and partly because trout in rivers – particularly those in clear-water streams – often seem to be more wary than those in stillwaters. While a 3 pound (roughly 0.15–0.18 mm) point is about right for trout and grayling fishing, it is necessary to go up to 8 to 10 pounds (0.25–0.30 mm) when fishing for sea trout. If in doubt, and especially if you are inexperienced, it is wise to err on the side of caution and to use a slightly heavier point rather than one that is too light. There is nothing sporting in fishing too fine and then leaving hooks in fishes' mouths when they break the line.

Droppers, used for wet-fly fishing, should be kept short and, where one is formed at a join between nylon of different strengths, it should be an extension of the stronger length.

Flies

Last on the list of truly essential items of equipment are the flies themselves. Trout flies can be divided into three main groups – imitative and food-suggesting patterns; traditional and attractor patterns; and lures. Imitative and food-suggesting patterns include all those designed to represent the various creatures that trout eat and those that, while not intended as specific imitations, look distinctly edible and are clearly taken by trout as food. There are many examples among the patterns listed as nymphs, emergers and dry flies on the first colour plate of flies, including the Black Superglue Buzzer, Terry's CDC Hawthorn, the Iron Blue Dun, the Blue-Winged Olive, Lunn's Spent Gnat and the Daddy Longlegs. Some imitative patterns, such as Sawyer's Pheasant Tail Nymph, the Hare's Ear and Amber Czech Mate, the CDC Hare's Ear and the Klinkhammer Light Olive, are used to deceive trout feeding on any one of an assortment of similar insects – the Pheasant Tail Nymph looks like the nymphs of many up-winged flies, the Czech Mate is shrimp- or nymph-like, and the CDC Hare's Ear and the Klinkhammer are both strongly suggestive of hatching or stillborn up-winged duns.

The food-suggesting patterns are very often dressed as spiders, with a few, sparse strands of hackle fibre swept back around a similarly sparse body. Simple and deadly, the patterns shown under the heading of Spider Patterns on the first colour plate of flies are all examples.

Imitative and food-suggesting patterns may be designed to float, sink or simply subside into the surface film. Floating flies have long been called dry flies and sinking ones wet flies; for the purposes of this book, I shall refer to the third group as emergers – the CDC Hare's Ear and the Klinkhammer Light Olive are both good examples.

Although some writers have sought to associate some traditional and attractor patterns with specific items of the trout's diet, these dressings are not, in fact, designed to represent or suggest any particular creature or group of creatures that fish eat. Such flies, almost all wet, are effective chiefly because they seem to pander to the trout's innate curiosity or aggression, and they are quite heavily stereotyped, most of them being similar in appearance, especially in silhouette. They almost all have slim, cylindrical or cigar-shaped bodies, feather-fibre tails, beard hackles, and stylized wings made of rolled mallard or teal feather fibre or of quill slips and angled back over their bodies. Examples of such patterns, which, on rivers, are mainly used for sea-trout fishing, include the first five sea-trout patterns shown in the second colour plate of flies, beginning with the Alexandra and ending with the Teal, Blue & Silver.

Lures, much beloved by many stillwater flyfishers, are patterns dressed on long-shank or tandem hooks, not intended to suggest or represent any part of the trout's diet. They are rarely used on streams or rivers, except for sea-trout fishing. The Mickey Finn, the Black Bumble and the Falkus Sunk Lure, all shown among the sea-trout patterns shown in the second colour plate of flies, are examples.

The Wading Staff

I include a wading staff among the list of more or less essential items not just because of the obvious advantages of having a third leg in fast or turbulent water, or when wading on rocky river beds, but because it can give one the confidence to fish otherwise inaccessible parts of a river. A wading staff should be weighted at its lower end. Ideally, it should have at least one short tungsten spike on its tip to reduce the risk of its skidding on slippery boulders. It should either be fitted with a long, looped lanyard, worn diagonally from one shoulder to the other side of the body, so that it can be released without drifting away, or with a wading staff retractor clipped to the waistcoat or wading belt.

Eye Protection

Polaroid sunglasses are essential, affording valuable protection to the eyes; a trout fly travelling back and forth past one's face at 30 or 40 mph is a very dangerous missile and, lodged in an eye, can do a great deal of damage. Polaroids also cut out glare from the water's surface, helping the angler to see into the water on clear-water streams, and thus to see fish.

The Priest

If fish are to be killed for the table, a priest – a small club with which to administer the last rites – is an essential part of the angler's tackle. If a trout has obliged us by accepting our offering and coming to the net, the least we owe it is the courtesy of a rapid and humane release from its discomfort. It is wholly unacceptable to leave a fish flapping on the bank while we go in search of a stick or stone with which to bludgeon it to death, or to try to hold it in our hands while we beat it against a fence post or some similarly unsuitable object. The priest, which may be bought or home-made, should be secured to the fishing waistcoat or belt by a length of cord to prevent its being lost.

Accessories

Beyond these bare essentials – a rod, a reel, a fly-line, a leader, a few flies, a wading staff, spectacles and a priest – there lies a whole range of more or less useful bits and pieces with which the flyfisher may or may not wish to burden himself.

A landing net is not an essential part of the river flyfisher's equipment. Unless one is fishing from a high bank, it is usually perfectly possible to land any trout by grasping it firmly across its back, immediately behind its gills, or to beach a sea trout. But most anglers find landing nets useful.

A landing net for use on streams and rivers should be light and unobtrusive when not in use, readily accessible when it is needed, reliable in operation and large enough to accommodate the biggest fish we may reasonably expect to catch. It must also have (by law) a woven or knitted mesh, rather than a knotted one, which can damage the mucous coating and scales that protect fish.

Except, perhaps, when sea-trout fishing at night, when it may double as a wading staff, there is no place on a stream or river for one of the vast long-handled landing nets that reservoir flyfishers are so fond of sticking into the ground beside them. The net I use has a large, rigid, bow-shaped frame and a telescopic handle. I sling it from a ring sewn high on to the back of my fishing waistcoat where I can get at it quickly and easily and where it is also well clear of brambles and barbed-wire fences. It has never let me down. The American tennis racket nets, slung on elasticized cord, are also good, particularly for small fish and for small-stream fishing.

Fly boxes may be simple tobacco tins, smart, sophisticated aluminium jobs with spring-lid compartments and neat rows of clips, or anything in between. The choice is yours. But whatever you use must be pocketable. Great wooden cases of flies should be left at home or in the car, serving only as repositories from which the small box or boxes in use may be replenished.

Although a small pair of blunt-nosed, serrated-edged scissors will prove invaluable for breaking down the barbs on hooks, trimming flies and cutting heavy nylon, a nipper will cut away waste nylon far closer to a knot than is possible with scissors. Most nippers also incorporate small spikes for clearing varnish from the eyes of hooks. Scissors and nippers can be hung from a zinger, one of those splendid little spring-loaded spools that can be pinned to a waistcoat and from which may be drawn 18 inches or so of cord with a clip on the end. Suspended thus, the tools will be ready to hand but will not get in the way.

Used flies returned wet to the confines of a fly box are liable to rust and to cause rust among others adjacent to them. A three– or four-inch-square patch of sheepskin pinned to shirt, pullover or waistcoat is ideal for holding them while they dry.

A few spare leaders or spools of nylon; a bottle of fly floatant; a piece of amadou in a folded leather holder for drying flies (amadou is a fungus with remarkable water-absorbing properties); a tub of the powder now widely available for perking up dry flies, completing the drying process and re-proofing them; a small tin of Mucilin leader floatant; a small tub of leader sinkant, made up at home from fuller's earth, glycerine and washing-up liquid, all mixed to a putty-like consistency; a marrow scoop and a small dish for examining the stomach contents of trout; perhaps, a hook hone for sharpening hooks; and an ordinary rubber eraser for straightening out nylon, should complete the tackle of even the most comprehensively equipped flyfisher. If that sounds a lot, it can actually all be stored away in or on a fishing waistcoat of quite modest capacity.

Tackle Assembly

Tackle assembly is largely a matter of common sense, but there are a few less obvious things that can be done to make it easier and to ensure that it all works as it should.

When you buy a new rod, its grip may well be covered with plastic sheathing which should be removed. It is only there to prevent the cork from becoming stained or discoloured while it is in the shop. If it is left on, the handle will be uncomfortable to hold and, more important, water will seep down between the plastic and the cork, which will eventually begin to rot.

It is worth rubbing the stub of a candle lightly over the male ferrules of the rod, to enable the joints to be pushed together smoothly, to ensure they do not come apart while you are fishing and to make them easier to take apart at the end of the day. The joints should not be pushed together too tightly – with a new rod, there should be a gap of just under a quarter of an inch once the joint has been properly made. The rings should be aligned carefully.

The reel should be seated securely and locked firmly into position. The line and leader should be led from it by the most direct route through the reel cage to the butt ring.

When threading the line and leader through the rings, it helps to lay the reel, handle up, on a flat, elevated surface, so that the rod is approximately horizontal. In this way, the line should not slip back through the rings if it is released accidentally during threading.

Once the rod has been put up, the tippet should be checked for soundness and the leader should be treated to float or to sink. If you want any part of the leader to float, smear it with a very thin layer of Mucilin, wipe your fingers and then wipe almost all of the Mucilin off. It takes only the minutest layer to keep the nylon afloat. The part of the leader you want to sink – perhaps all of it if you are sea-trout or upstream wet-fly fishing; perhaps just the front 18 inches or so for dry-fly or nymph fishing – should be very carefully rubbed down with a paste made of fuller's earth, washing-up liquid and glycerine (or any proprietary brand of sink aid), and then rinsed.

Tie a fly to the point of the tippet and secure it either to the little keeper ring immediately in front of the rod's handle or, as I do, take the leader around the back of the reel and up to one of the rod rings. This keeps the tip of the fly-line outside the tip ring making it easier to work out line when you begin to fish.

Finally, reluctant as I am to use the words always and never with regard to fishing, *always* carry your rod with the handle forwards and the point behind you. If you carry it pointing forwards while you are walking along, you risk digging it into the ground and breaking the tip. And *never* leave your rod lying flat on the ground, where someone is bound to tread on it eventually.

Clothing

Clothes worn for fly-fishing should be warm, comfortable, waterproof and, above all, unobtrusive to the fish. In all but the coldest weather, I generally wear a fishing waistcoat over a shirt or pullover. In its back pocket, I keep a very light and compact but fully waterproof nylon anorak.

When considering the colour and shade of clothing, it is important to take account of the kind of background against which you will be fishing. On open water, where the fish will see you against the sky, light grey or blue may be appropriate. Where you are likely to be fishing chiefly against a background of trees and bushes, mid to dark brown or green will be more suitable.

I would say that a broad-brimmed hat or cap is an essential part of the flyfisher's equipment. Apart from keeping you warm and helping to protect your head from fast-moving flies, the brim shades the eyes from the sun and, with the help of polaroid glasses, makes seeing into the water very much easier.

While it may sound extravagant, I have three pairs of waders, each of which meets the purpose for which I use it and none of which would serve the purpose for which I use the other pairs.

The first is a pair of lightweight thigh waders with cleated rubber soles, similar to those found on wellington boots. Wholly unsuitable for wading in anything but the gentlest of streams with the firmest of beds, I wear them almost exclusively for fishing the chalk streams. Here, they serve almost as much to keep my knees dry when kneeling and crawling as to keep my feet dry.

The second is a more robust pair of thigh waders, ideal for wading shallow, rocky streams. Their felt soles and tungsten studs provide a sure footing, even on smooth, algae-coated boulders, and they are quite rigid at the ankles, which reduces the risk of twists and sprains.

The third is a pair of breathable, stocking-foot chest waders, which I use when fishing deeper rivers. They are worn with lightweight, felt-soled, tungsten studded wading boots. Early breathable waders had a tendency to spring leaks. Good-quality modern ones seem not to (mine have been quite heavily used for five seasons now), and they offer a very considerable advantage over the alternative, neoprene, in that they can be folded very small for packing and travelling.

Chest waders should never be used without a wading belt – a simple canvas belt that prevents them from filling with water if you take a ducking – or without gravel guards – gaiters, to prevent gravel from infiltrating between the boot and the wader foot, potentially puncturing the latter.

5 To Cast a Trout Fly

The only real short-cut to competent casting is to seek instruction from a qualified game-angling coach. The cost is generally modest and the rewards are enormous. After half a dozen one-hour lessons with a qualified game-angling instructor you may expect to be able to cast respectable distances, confidently, accurately and without undue effort, which is the object of the exercise. Even those who have been fishing for some time can benefit from a lesson or two from time to time, to iron out faults that have become habitual and to learn new casting and fishing techniques.

Game-angling instruction in the UK is overseen by an umbrella organization, the Game-angling Instructors' Association (GIA), which works closely with the Salmon & Trout Association, the governing body for game angling. The GIA was formed quite recently through the amalgamation of a number of instructional bodies, and its members may have qualifications awarded by the Advanced Professional Game Angling Instructors' Association (APGAI) or the Register of Experienced Fly Fishing Instructors and Guides (REFFIS), or they may hold the Salmon & Trout Association National Instructors' Certificate (STANIC) or the Scottish Game Anglers Instructors' Certificate (SGAIC). I would strongly advise newcomers to seek instruction from someone with at least one of these qualifications. All other ways of learning to cast and to fish have serious inherent pitfalls.

Anyone may set themselves up as a game-angling instructor but the unqualified, who may well be self-taught and have not had their knowledge, casting and teaching skills reviewed by any recognized body, are more than likely to have serious faults of their own and to pass them on to their students.

Being taught by family and friends is even more hazardous; not only will they pass on their faults but they tend also to be less than single-minded in their approach to instruction. Typically, having arrived at the waterside, the well-meaning friend will start you off, spend ten or fifteen minutes trying to correct your faults and then, eager to get fishing, wander off, leaving you to practise whatever you may or may not have been taught.

Trying to teach yourself through trial and error, perhaps with the assistance of video lessons or the written word, is an even more uncertain and laborious process, which raises questions about this chapter. There are, however, some people who are unable to obtain professional advice for one reason or another, and others who, while perhaps unwilling to seek formal instruction, may be prepared to look critically at their own casting and try to improve it. For these people, I believe it is worth considering the principles involved in casting a trout fly, pointing to some of the commonest casting faults and explaining how they may be corrected.

Effective casting has everything to do with timing and technique and nothing whatever to do with brute strength.

In coarse and sea fishing, anglers become accustomed to using their relatively stiff rods as levers with which to throw quite heavy terminal tackle – baited hooks, split shot or leads, floats, and so on – out over the water. A trout fly and the leader to which it is attached weigh virtually nothing and cannot be thrown any distance. So, in complete contrast to the way in which coarse and sea-fishing rods are used, a fly rod is used chiefly as a spring, loading it with the weight of the fly-line so that it fires the line, and the leader and fly attached to it, out over the water. I say chiefly because engineers and physicists will point out, quite rightly, that a fly rod is actually a combination of lever and spring. In learning to cast, though, it helps greatly to think of it simply as a spring. If this fundamental principle is accepted – as it must be if progress is to be made with casting – then a number of other essential truths follow from it.

First, a fly rod cannot be expected to work efficiently without a reasonable amount of line out beyond the tip ring – 10 or 12 yards is the ideal to start with. Much less and you will have nothing with which to load the rod.

Second, by far the greater part of the effort we put into casting must go into the up-cast, to load the spring. Power for the forward cast must come very largely from the energy thus stored in the rod rather than from the angler.

Third, the further the rod is taken back beyond the vertical on the up-cast, the less efficiently will it work as a spring.

Fourth, the line must be given sufficient time to straighten out behind the angler on the up-cast if it is fully to load the rod in preparation for the forward cast.

The Overhead Cast

So, for a simple, straightforward, overhead cast, the aim is to extend at least 10 yards of line beyond the rod tip, to lift it into a high, fast up-cast, to pause to allow the line to straighten in the air behind you, loading the rod, and then to give the rod a forward tap, directing the line out over the water.

If you are a beginner, it will pay you to do your initial casting practice on grass, where you can concentrate on the job in hand without having half your attention diverted by the possibility of catching fish and where there is no water movement to complicate things. Instead of a fly, tie a small tuft of wool to the end of your leader. If you tie on nothing at all, the leader it will crackle in the air and accumulate knots.

Start by pulling about 10 yards of line out beyond the rod tip. How you hold the rod is very largely a matter of personal choice. Grip it comfortably in the middle of the handle. Some people elect to have the V between forefinger and thumb uppermost, as I do; others prefer to have the thumb on top. The grip you may occasionally see, with the index finger extended along the top of the handle, causes the rod to be held with the last three fingers rather than chiefly with the index and middle ones, which is inefficient. Whatever grip you use, the butt of the rod should be tucked up quite tightly beneath your wrist.

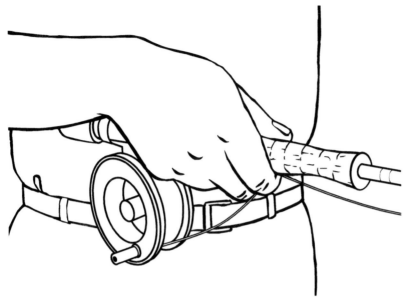

Fig. 13 The most effective rod grip
(Note that the 'V' between the forefinger and thumb is on top of the handle,
and that the butt of the handle is tucked up quite tightly beneath the wrist)

For the moment, trap the line against the handle of the rod with your index finger.

How you position your feet is also a matter of choice. The greater part of your casting from the bank on streams and rivers will, or should, be done from a kneeling position, anyway. But there is some advantage in putting the right foot or knee forward if you are right-handed (the left for left-handers) as it helps to prevent the development of a throwing action – by far the commonest characteristic of bad casting.

Much nonsense used to be talked about keeping the elbow into the side while casting, some people even advocating tucking a book in between the elbow and the rib cage to prevent the elbow from wandering away. In truth, successful casting has much to do with being comfortable and relaxed, neither of which is encouraged by so unnaturally rigid a discipline. What is important is to do most of the work with the biceps, elbow and forearm, rather than extending the whole arm and working from the shoulder, which inevitably makes for loss of control.

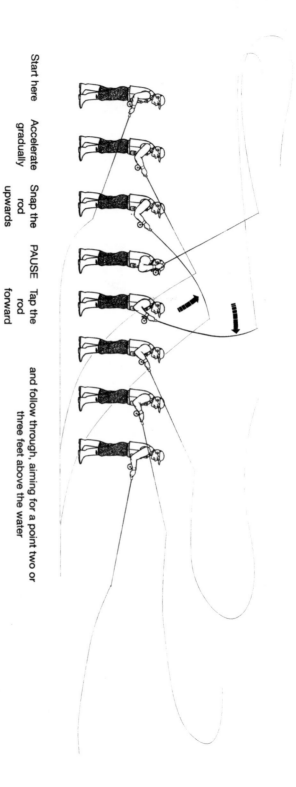

Start here   Accelerate   Snap the   PAUSE   Tap the   and follow through, aiming for a point two or
         gradually   rod   rod   three feet above the water
                upwards   forward

Fig. 14 The overhead cast

Start the up-cast with the rod tip close to the ground and lift the rod, quite slowly at first, accelerating through the 10 o'clock position, snapping it up to about 12 o'clock as the tip of the fly-line leaves the water, pushing the line up high and fast behind you. In terms of fore- and upper-arm movement, the action involved is not dissimilar to that used in preparing to throw a dart, with the hand being raised to the eye.

You should aim to stop the rod at about 12 o'clock (it will inevitably drift back to between 1 and 2 o'clock, but should be allowed to go no further), and the butt should not be allowed to break away from the wrist by more than about 1½ inches. If you find this difficult at first, wind a velcro-fastened cloth strap around your wrist and the butt of the rod. One of the most widespread casting faults is allowing the rod to drift too far back on the up-cast, often because the butt is allowed to break far too far away from the wrist.

At the top of the up-cast, pause, and do not be afraid to do so. If you have achieved a high, fast up-cast, you will be surprised at how long you can pause without the slightest risk of the line or your fly sagging behind you – a full second, at least, with 10 yards of line out. You *must* pause to allow the line to straighten in the air. If you do not, at best the rod will be under insufficient tension to enable you to execute a good forward cast and, at worst, you will crack your fly off.

Now, simply give the rod a forward tap, just as if you were throwing a dart at a board no more than 10 feet away, and follow through, extending your arm slightly and pointing the rod at a spot 3 feet above your target.

Perhaps the second most widespread casting fault is putting too much effort into the forward cast. As we have already seen, a fly and fly-line cannot be thrown. If you try to throw them you will decrease rather than increase your casting distance, the leader will land on the water in a heap and you will put knots into it – euphemistically called wind knots but, in fact, always bad-casting knots.

For the most elementary river fishing, that is all that is required – 10 yards of line, a steady lift and acceleration, a pause and a tap forward. But, for working the line out and in order to remove the moisture from a dry fly, it is necessary to be able to false cast. The basic movements are exactly the same as for a simple, single, overhead cast, except that line is drawn from the reel into the left hand and held there, to be released at the end of the forward cast or in increasing amounts over a succession of forward casts.

For beginners, the interim step between a single cast and a series of false casts is to start once again with 10 yards of line out beyond the rod tip. Pull 5 or 6 feet back through the butt ring of the rod and hold it lightly with the left hand so that the length from your hand to the butt ring is reasonably taut and the length from your hand to the reel is slack. The left hand should be kept by your side; it *must not* follow the rod up as you start the up-cast.

Now, do a simple cast – steady lift, accelerate to the vertical, allow a slight backwards drift, pause, tap forward – and while you are following through, release the line with your left hand. Provided that you release it at the right moment, the slack line will be pulled out through the rod rings by the weight of the line already beyond the tip ring. If you release the line too early, you will hear a nasty hissing sound as you pull the rings down the line rather than allow the line to glide out through them. If you release it too late, the power of the cast will have been dissipated and the slack line will not be pulled out.

Your objective is to extend the line out over the water and then to allow it to drop gently on to the surface. If it splashes on to the water (or thumps on to the grass), or if it is going out too high and then falling untidily back towards you, remind yourself to aim for a point 2 or 3 feet above the water's surface.

Incidentally, whenever you are casting, whether in practice or when you are actually fishing, you should always select a target to aim for; if there is no obvious fish to cast to, pick out a leaf, or a ripple, or a particular eddy, or even just a reflection on the surface, and aim at it. Only thus will you be able to cast consistently accurately when you need to.

When you are confident that you can extend 5 or 6 feet of line through the rod rings, you can go on to full, repetitive false casting. The action is exactly the same – lift, accelerate, drift, pause, tap forward, release line through the left hand. Now, though, you simply check the rod at about the 11 o'clock position on the forward cast and pause again, allowing the line to extend in front of you, before gripping it again and accelerating the rod back into a second, third or fourth up-cast.

Lift, accelerate backwards and upwards, drift, pause . . . tap forward, release line, pause . . . re-grip line, accelerate backwards and upwards, drift . . . tap forward and release line.

When extending line by false casting, it can only be released on the forward cast, after the forward tap. If you try to release it at any other stage, it will go out of control and land in an embarrassing heap around your ears.

When fishing – and, indeed, in practice – it is important to remember that a fly-line flickering back and forth through the air is very visible from beneath the water's surface and can easily alarm fish. False casting should therefore be kept to an absolute minimum. It is perfectly possible to extend 15 or 20 yards of line with no more than three or four false casts, and your objective should be to do so.

The Side Cast

This brings us quite naturally to the side cast – a little more difficult than the overhead cast but very much less likely to frighten fish, especially on clear-water streams.

We saw in Chapter 2 that light passing into water is refracted downwards, the extent to which it bends increasing as its angle of attack on the surface of the water becomes lower. As a consequence, objects on the bank seen from underwater appear to be shorter and fatter than they actually are, and something like a fishing rod held vertically becomes markedly more obvious than we might suspect, especially when waved back and forth, quite probably flashing in the light. However, if you cast in a horizontal plane rather than a vertical one, the rod may well disappear below the edge of the fish's window and, even if it does not, will become far less visible from beneath the water.

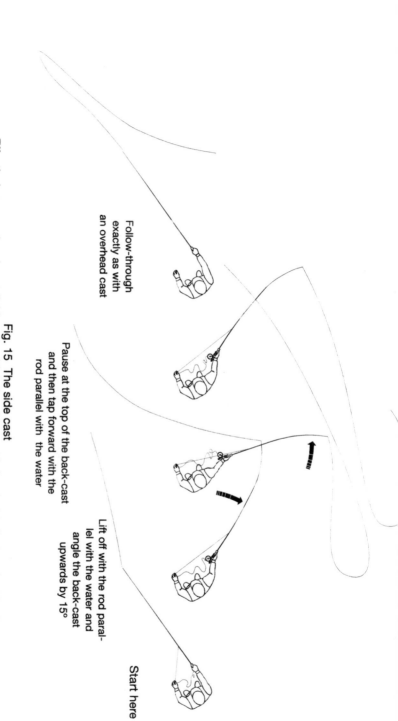

Follow-through
exactly as with
an overhead cast

Pause at the top of the back-cast
and then tap forward with the
rod parallel with the water

Lift off with the rod parallel with the water and
angle the back-cast
upwards by 15°

Start here

Fig. 15 The side cast

Effectively an overhead cast 'laid on its side', the side cast is invaluable for keeping the fly
rod out of the fish's field of vision, but it takes practice to achieve consistent accuracy with it

The action of the side cast is almost exactly the same as that used for the overhead cast but with the rod held horizontally. The rod is raised slightly on the up-cast in order to lift the line, lowered to the horizontal during the pause there and then tapped forward parallel with the ground or water.

The two difficulties of the side cast are keeping the line high enough to avoid catching grass and other vegetation behind you, and achieving accuracy.

The solution to the first of these problems is to put a little more energy into the up-cast and to angle it slightly upwards, accelerating the line high and fast behind you. The answer to the second is less easy and chiefly has to do with practice. A rod moved back and forth in a vertical plane will, inevitably, deliver a line in the direction in which it is pointed, provided that there is no unduly fierce side wind. However, if a rod is moved to and fro in a horizontal plane, the line – and the fly attached to it – are as likely to swing off to left or right as they are to land where you want them to. Side-casting accuracy cannot be taught through the written word; it is a matter of practice and perseverance. But the effort, if you are prepared to make it, should be amply rewarded by a significant increase in the number of fish you catch.

The Roll Cast

The third type of cast essential to stream and river flyfishers is the roll cast, used both to extend line where trees or bushes behind you make an up-cast impracticable, and to bring an intermediate, a sinking or a sink-tip line to the surface so that it may be lifted into a normal up-cast. The roll cast is simple to perform but can only be practised on water as it relies to a large extent on the surface tension for its successful execution.

With 10 yards or so of line on the water, lift the rod quite slowly to about the 1 o'clock position and tip it away from you slightly. There is no hurry in this phase of the cast; the object is to put the rod into a position where the line will hang down in a bow behind it before curving forward into or on to the water.

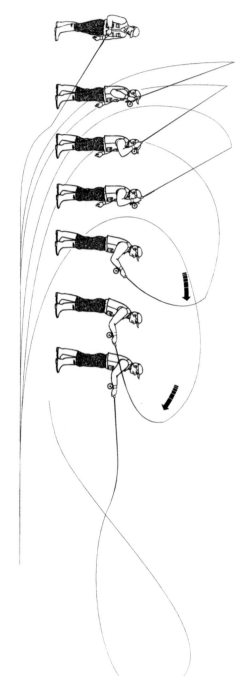

Start with
the rod tip
low

Lift slowly until the
line forms a 'D'
behind the rod

Hit the rod down
HARD

Follow through, aiming at a point
about three feet above the
water's surface

Fig. 16 The roll-cast

Now, bang the rod down hard towards the water in front of you with all the force you would use to hammer a nail into a board at waist level, bringing it to a stop at about the 10 o'clock position.

To start with, it takes a little courage to beat your possibly new and precious rod downwards in this way, but you will do it no harm and, assuming you apply enough force, the line should, apparently magically, lift back towards you and then roll out over the water. With a little practice, you should be able to put out 15 yards or so of line quite accurately in this way.

Tricks and Wrinkles

Preventing drag

Drag refers to the skidding of a fly across the surface, almost always caused by the current pulling on fly-line and leader, and preventing it is one of the dry-flyfisher's most constant challenges. Fish rarely take dragging flies, even though the drag may be imperceptible.

Drag can often be prevented by casting very accurately, so that the fly only has to drift the shortest possible distance before it reaches the fish, giving the current little time to interfere with its sedate progress, and by putting a little slack into the cast. This can be achieved either by a very slight lift of the rod tip just before the fly alights on the water or by a gentle tug on the fly-line with the left hand at that same point.

Casting into the wind

The wind is the flyfisher's most persistent adversary. However competent a caster may be, it is never as easy to cast into a headwind or across a brisk side wind as it is to put out a line downwind. But it is perfectly possible to cast into or across a stiff breeze and, once again, the principles involved have everything to do with technique and nothing whatever to do with brute strength.

Those who do not understand the mechanics of casting almost always do battle with the wind by trying to *throw* the line into it, putting more and more effort into the forward cast. But we have already established that you cannot throw a fly-line any distance, even in calm air; less still can you do so with the wind against you. The harder you try to throw the line, the more will it land in an untidy heap on the water in front of you, and the more frustrated will you become.

The key to beating the wind is to load the rod more by increasing line speed on the up-cast, stopping the rod nearer the vertical than you would normally, with less backward drift, and then tapping forward to project the line low and fast across the water – being careful to resist the temptation to put extra force into the forward tap.

Changing direction

There are two ways of changing direction while casting, one ungainly, time consuming and potentially fish frightening, the other quick and efficient. Most self-taught flyfishers use the former – lifting the line from the water and then moving around about 5 degrees with each successive false cast. The infinitely preferable alternative is to point the rod at the target *before* lifting the line from the water and then simply to cast as normal. The line will be virtually on course for the new target as it straightens at the top of the up-cast, and one false cast should have it aimed precisely.

Cutting corners

There are times when you may need to put a steep curve into the fly-line as it lands on the water. The trick is particularly useful when casting to fish tucked in beneath the bank from which you are fishing, or lurking under an overhanging bush or tree.

There is nothing difficult about this, although casting an accurate and predictable curve does require a little practice. Simply make a perfectly ordinary overhead cast and then, as soon as you have tapped forward, drop the rod to the horizontal – to the right or the left – in the opposite direction to the one in which you want the line to curve. If you want the line to curve to the left, tip the rod to the right, and *vice versa*.

Problem Solving

Most of the problems people have with their casting are caused by a small number of very common faults.

The line crawls towards you and fails to get into the air on the up-cast: you have not been positive enough in accelerating the line into the up-cast. The acceleration should be progressive and the movement from about 10.30 to the top of the cast should be quite brisk.

The line leaps from the water but still fails to climb into the up-cast: you are snatching the line from the water rather than accelerating it into the up-cast progressively.

The fly catches an obstruction behind you or hits you in the back as it travels forwards: you are making a back-cast rather than an up-cast, taking the rod too far back, very probably because you are allowing your wrist to break too much at the top of the cast. At the end of the up-cast, the line will continue to move in the direction the rod tip was moving when it stopped. The problem can be solved by making sure the rod tip is still moving upwards at the top of the up-cast.

The power is dissipated from the rod as you tap forward when shooting line, or the cast falls short of an attainable target: you are probably releasing the line too soon; tap forward and *then* release the line.

The line crashes on to the water's surface: you are aiming *at* the target, rather than 2 or 3 feet *above* it; aim at a point above the target.

You keep getting wind knots in the leader, or the line hits the ground or the water in front of you during false casting: you have resorted to a throwing action, either because, perhaps subconsciously, you believe it will enable you to cast further – which it most certainly will not – or because you are allowing your wrist to break too much at the top of the up-cast. Discipline your wrist, reducing the amount the butt of the rod is allowed to break from it, and concentrate on getting a high, fast up-cast.

You hear a whiplash crack as you go into the forward cast; perhaps the fly even snaps off from the end of your leader: you are starting the forward tap too early, before the fly-line has had time to extend at the top of the up-cast. *Pause* at the top of the up-cast.

The fly or the fly-line catches on the rod during false casting: you are almost certainly moving the rod fore and aft through too narrow an arc. While checking it at 12 o'clock on the up-cast, allow the rod to drift back to between 1 and 2 o'clock, and allow it to drift forward to between 10 and 11 o'clock on the forward cast.

The line leaps from the water and then falls in a heap during the first movement of a roll cast: you have carried out the movement too quickly and forcefully. It should be a slow, deliberate action.

The line fails to extend fully and to roll out over the water during a roll cast: you are not making the downward hit with the rod sharply or strongly enough; it must be a crisp, positive action.

Finally, do remember that the keys to good casting are timing, technique and an understanding of the mechanical principles involved, rather than the brute force and ignorance so often demonstrated by self-taught or badly taught anglers. Remember, too, that good casting does not come naturally, especially to those used to throwing things or casting with coarse or sea-fishing rods. Anyone can cast badly, lashing the water to a foam, half-hurling themselves into the river with each forward cast, accumulating a mass of knots in their leaders as they do so. Effortless accuracy and delicacy come only with practice.

snippers

tippet material

fly floatant

Mucilin

leader sinkant

spring balance

priest

rod licence and fishing permit

fly patch

polarized sunglasses

forceps

fly box

The river fly fisher's paraphernalia

Wading requires caution and a wading staff secured by a cord across the shoulder

Early season on the River Torridge; fish will often be found beneath steep, undercut banks

Fishing the head of a pool; trout will often be found in the slack water beside a more turbulent current

Trout often lie in the slack water at the tail of a pool, but drag can pose problems for the angler

The perfect lie – in the slack water immediately above a natural groyne in the river

It is better to pull line from the reel and arrange it on the bank before starting
to cast rather than to lengthen line while false casting

Overhanging trees and bushes provide trout with cover and a steady supply
of food, even early in the season

Trout find a plentiful supply of food immediately downstream from cattle drinks, where cows stir up the river bed

Good fish may often be found in a streamy run between a weed bed and the bank

Larger than average trout will often be found tight in against the bank just below the inflow of a side-stream

It is essential to carry out a daylight reconnaissance of any sea trout pool you plan to fish at night

It should come as no surprise that the biggest fish are often to be found under the lowest bridges

When playing a fish, keep low and keep the rod tip up

If a fish is to be returned, there should be no need to net it or touch it; simply run your hand down the leader and ease the hook out

When netting a fish, don't scoop at it, just draw it steadily over the rim of the net

6 Of Times and Seasons

There is not much to be said for going fishing when the fish are not feeding or, worse still, heading off in pursuit of sea trout when there are no sea trout to be had. Obvious as this may seem, it is astonishing how many people forget it, allowing themselves to succumb to domestic pressure to do this or that in the morning, simply grabbing a couple of hours at the riverside in the afternoon, or allowing dinner at eight to drag them away before the evening rise. Even some fishing hotels are unhelpful in this respect, being reluctant to arrange early dinners or to leave out late suppers for those who want to fish through the evenings in the summer. It can be tempting, also, to arrange a visit to, say, Wales or the West Country in mid June in the hope of catching a few early sea trout whereas, in reality, there is no likelihood that they will arrive in significant numbers until the beginning of July. We cannot expect consistent success if the timing of fishing trips is dictated by human convenience or wishful thinking, rather than by the habits of the quarry.

It is not only the interests of others or personal convenience that can cause the stream or river flyfisher to sally forth at unproductive times. Those who come to running water from lakes and reservoirs often apply the timings they are used to on stillwaters to their new surroundings, but the two can be very different.

Through most of the season – certainly from May to September – stillwater trout tend to feed early and late, a graph of their activity rising steadily for the first couple of hours after dawn, falling away through the rest of the morning to a flat period in the afternoon and then, one hopes, rising steeply again at dusk. Apart from the variations caused by major changes in the weather, this pattern is fairly consistent. Only at the beginning and end of the season may the fish be expected to feed throughout the day. Keen stillwater flyfishers tend therefore to be early risers, heading for the water at sun-up. When they come to streams and rivers, they must learn to curb their impatience. In some ways, trout – and, indeed, grayling – in running water are more civilized than their counterparts in lakes and reservoirs, rising late and rarely showing much interest in flies, natural or artificial, before midmorning. Frustratingly, they actually do a great deal of their feeding at night, when dry-fly and nymph fishing is impracticable. But that is another story.

Trout in running water feed on a rather greater variety of invertebrates than stillwater trout do, and those invertebrates differ quite widely in their habits. Therefore the behaviour patterns of these trout vary rather more than do those of trout in lakes and reservoirs, and it is worth going through the season stage by stage to consider the changes in the fishes' behaviour and the factors that cause them. It should be emphasized, though, that these observations are general. Extremes of weather can alter patterns or even postpone them for as much as two or three weeks.

Early Season

The opening date of the trout season varies throughout the British Isles, generally being earlier in the west (mid February in Ireland, early to mid March in Wales and the West Country) than in the east, where the river flyfisher has to wait until mid April or even early May before he may cast a line.

Where the season opens in February or March, it is more of an acknowledgement of impending spring than an invitation to fish. The water is likely still to be swollen and cold, with little fly in evidence, and brown trout are still recovering from spawning. While warm weather may produce occasional hatches at this time of year, the fish should not be expected to come to the fly enthusiastically until mid to late April.

In April, the successful flyfisher will be one who is prepared to cancel or postpone lunch. The two main up-winged fly species of interest to trout, and therefore to anglers, are the march brown (on spate rivers, chiefly in Wales, Scotland and the west of England) and the large dark olive, which is found almost everywhere. Both appear, often in large numbers, from about 11.30 in the morning until about 2 or 2.30 in the afternoon, but are almost completely absent at other times.

The march brown nymph shows a marked preference for well-oxygenated water and hatches are usually quite localized, being confined to fast, turbulent stretches of river and the areas immediately downstream of them. The large dark olive is less demanding and hatches may occur anywhere. But, early in the season, and especially on the chalk streams, it seems to be very temperature-dependent. In very cold weather, a slight softening of the air can trigger a hatch, as can a chill breeze springing up during a warm, muggy period. Under such conditions, hatches can be quite brief, lasting for no more than perhaps twenty minutes or so, but they can provide excellent sport when they do occur.

Also widespread but localized is the Grannom, the earliest-hatching of the caddis flies. Most other caddis species hatch in the evenings, but this early season one is very much a middle-of-the-day creature, and so enthusiastically do the trout welcome it that it would be foolish indeed to be at home or in the pub when it appears.

Towards the end of April, flyfishers in Scotland, Ireland and the north of England reap the benefits bestowed by the earliest stoneflies. The first to appear is the generically named large dark stonefly, hatches of which continue into June. The hatch itself, which occurs during the night, is of little interest to the trout; it is the arrival of the egg-laying females on the water throughout the day and into the evening that arouses the fish.

On many streams and rivers, the last week in April and the first in May offer the first reliable morning fishing of the year, provided by the hawthorn fly. The hawthorn, a terrestrial insect, is sometimes described as being unreliable both in its appearance and in its appeal to the fish. My own experience leads me to disagree entirely; it has provided me with many marvellous mornings on rivers all over the country. It is true that it can be a little frustrating to watch numbers of hawthorn flies (rarely 'clouds' of them), with their jet-black bodies and gangling legs, hovering around bankside trees and bushes and never apparently being blown on to the water. But it only takes a few of them to whet the trout's appetite, and once the fish have developed a taste for them they will usually take a matching artificial with great enthusiasm whether the naturals are actually on the water or not.

It may be that those who regard the hawthorn as unreliable do so because its season is so very short and because they have tended to arrive by the river late in the morning, when the fall is petering out. The last few days in April and the first few in May are the only ones in the season during which I make a conscientious effort to be on the water by 9 or 9.30, armed with half a dozen or so artificial hawthorn flies.

May and June

The transformation seen on our streams and rivers between the end of April and the middle of May can be astonishing. In the space of no more than a fortnight, problems of scarcity of fly life are, or should be, replaced by those posed by superabundance, both in terms of the range of species available to the fish and of the numerical sizes of the hatches. I say 'or should be' because the recent alarming decline in fly numbers, especially on the chalk streams, is never more evident than at this time of year.

The large dark olive of spring is superseded by the medium olive throughout England and Scotland and by the olive upright in Scotland, Wales, Ireland and the north of England. Although the medium olive can appear at any time of day, my own impression is that it most commonly does so from mid to late morning until mid afternoon and then again around teatime. The olive upright is very much a creature of the evening.

May is also the time for the iron blue, that tiny, dark, up-winged fly so beloved of fish and fishermen alike. It seems almost to relish the cold, squally showers we sometimes get at this time of year, hatches becoming increasingly prolific as the weather becomes fouler, great armadas of the little insects riding out the storm, providing rich pickings for hungry trout, and sometimes for tenacious fishermen under what often seem to be the most unpropitious conditions. Although hatches of iron blues are said to occur at any time of day, I do not recall having seen one before about 10.30 or 11 in the morning and, again, the best of them have generally been around lunchtime and during the afternoons.

Milder mid May days may be the time for the first falls of that other useful terrestrial insect, the black gnat. Given the decline in aquatic fly numbers, and the mayfly aside, artificials tied to represent the black gnat and its smaller look-alike, the reed smut, can be great stand-bys, often providing the only reasonably reliable dry-fly fishing to be had from May onwards.

During May evenings, the first significant midge hatches are likely to occur. They will continue throughout the rest of the season and can be very appealing to both trout and grayling. I suspect hatching midge pupae may cause some confusion among flyfishers who presume evening rises always to be to up-winged spinners or to sedges.

Especially on the chalk streams, but elsewhere, too, all this activity is largely eclipsed by the arrival of the mayfly in mid May. Fortunately, mayfly populations seem relatively immune to whatever it is that has been eroding the numbers of other aquatic up-winged fly species. So spectacular and fascinating are the mayflies that they have been studied in detail and at length by every angling entomologist, and most flyfishers well understand their essential characteristics.

Although a few individual duns may be seen from late April or early May onwards, the mayfly hatch proper starts in southern England quite precisely between 15 and 21 or 22 May. It continues until the second week in June, when it begins to peter out. On a small number of fisheries, mayflies may continue to appear in significant numbers, and the fish to take them, right up until the end of June. As is the case with most up-winged flies, occasional individual specimens may be seen in almost any month of the year. The latest I have seen a mayfly hatching has been in October. But only very rarely do trout and grayling take any notice of such maverick, out-of-season flies, which should be seen as no more than oddities.

During the mayfly season, the duns – large and wholly unmistake-able – may hatch from about midday onwards but are generally most numerous in the mid- and late afternoon, and falls of the bright, shin-ing spinners are most evident in the evenings, from about six o'clock.

It has been said, and it seems to be true, that the best of the mayfly fishing is to be had four days into the hatch, when the trout have had time to become used to the sheer size and quantity of the insects, and again a few days before the hatch ends.

During the mayfly season – and especially through the middle part of it – it is worth remembering that the other insect species are still hatching and that the trout can, and often will, turn to them as a side dish. Only too often has one persisted with an artificial mayfly and wasted good fishing time in pursuit of a trout that eventually proved to be preoccupied with medium olives, iron blues or even midge pupae.

Above all others, the mayfly hatch illustrates perfectly the need for self-discipline and restraint. It happens at the prettiest time of year when most of us would wish to spend the whole day on the water; and it happens when many other fly species are, or should be, much in evidence. The urge to be on the water by ten o'clock in the morning and to make a day of it can be difficult to resist. The risk, however, is that you will potter around during the morning and early afternoon, pick-ing up fish here and there on black gnats, iron blues or the like, and have caught as many as you are allowed by the time the mayfly hatch begins at teatime.

The end of the mayfly hatch sees a dramatic reduction in activity. Some chalk-stream anglers have attributed this to the trout having gorged themselves on mayflies, but that is patent nonsense. The truth is that such daytime hatches as there may be from mid June onwards tend to be sparse and spasmodic, spread thinly throughout the day, and, for the time being, determined morning and afternoon rises to hordes of surface flies are a thing of the past.

For all this, and for all the sad talk about the 'dog days', there is still a wide range of insects available to the fish and there are still fish to be had. An artificial daddy-long-legs can work wonders throughout the summer, eliciting rises from fish that may appear to be wholly uninterested in surface feeding. Occasional fish may be found feeding busily on reed smuts or other minute surface insects. Equally, you may need to fish a nymph or even a deep-sunk shrimp through the day, and you may well have to cancel dinner in the evening, for that is when the fishing is likely to be at its best.

Although the medium olive and the olive upright are still about, if in somewhat smaller numbers than hitherto, and the pale watery and the cinnamon sedge will have started to appear on the water in the late afternoons, hatches can be sparse and unpredictable, and any real expectation of success must be reserved for the evening rise, which is by no means always reliable. If you are lucky, it may last for up to an hour before darkness; at least as often, it will be over in five or ten minutes; sometimes it will simply not happen at all.

July and August

In his marvellous book *A Summer on the Test*, John Waller Hills placed July at the head of his list of favourite fishing months, chiefly because it provided him with the most exacting test of his skill. Newcomers to streams and rivers and those who cannot pick and choose when they will fish because of work and family commitments may disagree with him, for this is undoubtedly the most difficult time of year. These are the heavy, often humid days of high summer. The leaves on the trees have lost the lightness of spring and the undergrowth – thistles, nettles, cow parsley and brambles – is tall, dense, ensnaring and unforgiving. Streams and rivers are at their lowest, often with a languid lifelessness about them that can dent confidence even before you begin, and good bags of trout are hard to come by.

But it is a time, too, when experimentation, observation and opportunism can be richly rewarded. Occasional good fish taken against the odds can be far more satisfying than any number of easy ones.

In the daytime, you should not expect to see widespread hatches of flies, with every fish in the river rising to them. Search, instead, for the odd maverick trout, tucked in beneath a bush and coming up to falling caterpillars or beetles. Spend time on the leviathan who has been lurking in the shade under a low bridge since the season began, often bypassed by anglers who branded him uncatchable and concentrated their attentions on easier quarry. Try trundling a deep-sunk shrimp or nymph down long, deep runs or through the dark water of a hatch pool. Watch for falls of ants or black gnats and be prepared to take advantage of their often brief appearances. Look out for cinnamon sedges close against the reeds and rushes in the afternoons, and for individual trout showing interest in them. And wait for the evening.

There is something wonderfully gentle about an evening at the waterside in high summer. The air is often heavy and still, deadening all but the most local sounds. There is promise in the appearance of the first few pale wateries, blue winged olives, midges and sedges, and in the occasional early rise at seven or so, which seems so certainly to presage a more general and productive one later on. Indeed it may, but it may forewarn of some of the most frustrating fishing imaginable, too. However sure we are that we know what the trout are feeding on, persuading them to take our copies can often be quite extraordinarily difficult on summer evenings. The answer – far from certain, but at least good for one's peace of mind if not necessarily for the creel – is to keep calm, to avoid over-inflating expectations and to watch the water very carefully.

Late in the evening, the fish are likely to be taking either spent spinners, midge pupae hanging right in the surface film, or sedges, and to be wholly preoccupied with one specific insect. The noisy, sometimes explosive rise to a sedge is usually self-explanatory, but rises to spinners and midge pupae can be very similar. If the trout consistently refuse your Lunn's Particular or Sherry Spinner, try them with a small (size 14 or 16) Black Superglue Buzzer.

If July and August can be frustrating for those who fish for non-migratory trout, they more than make up for it with the sea-trout fishing they offer. As we saw in Chapter 2, British sea-trout runs begin in earnest in July and continue through September. Sea-trout fishing is considered in detail in Chapter 10 but it is worth noting here that they, too, call for restraint. While sea trout can be caught during the daytime and often are, their wariness argues for fishing for them chiefly at night. Heading for the water as dusk closes in, it can be very tempting to start fishing too early, alarming every fish in the pool. It can take a high level of self-discipline to wait until it is pitch dark before making the first cast, but that is what you must do if you are to give yourself the best possible chance of success.

September

With its soft days, light breezes and excellent fly hatches, September compensates the flyfisher for the difficulties faced in July and August. Sport can now be as good as it was in mid May and, as the evenings draw in, we may go out in the daytime with reasonable expectations of success.

Pale wateries are likely to appear at any time from late morning onwards, as are medium olives and iron blue duns, last seen in quantity in the spring. There may be some sedges about in the daytime, although the caperer, well imitated by William Lunn's artificial of the same name, is a creature of the evening, as are the blue-winged olive and its spinner, the sherry spinner.

October, November and December

For those who extend their seasons into the autumn and early winter by going in pursuit of grayling, fly hatches and their timings become increasingly like those seen in March and April as October gives way to November. Large dark olives, last seen in large numbers in late April or early May, often reappear strongly throughout the country in October, usually around lunchtime or in the early afternoons. The iron blue dun should still be much in evidence in October, particularly on cold, blustery days; and we may expect to see pale watery duns and spinners through until the beginning of November, chiefly in the late afternoons.

By mid November, though, the flies of our streams and rivers will be drawing the curtains on the year, the nymphs becoming increasingly dormant and disinclined to hatch. Apart from very occasional flurries of activity on mild days and the odd hatch of midges, the insect life of the river will have put itself to bed for the winter, and we shall find ourselves compelled to rely on deep-sunk shrimp patterns and fancy dry flies, which may bring the fish up even when there are few if any naturals on the water.

7 Dry-Fly Fishing

Of the four main methods of fly-fishing – dry-fly fishing, nymph fishing, upstream wet-fly fishing, and wet-fly fishing across and down – none is in any way superior to the others. Each has its time and place. Dry-fly and nymph fishing are practised on most streams and rivers and are, to some degree, interchangeable, dry flies being fished to surface-feeding trout and grayling, or at least to fish we believe we may be able to tempt to the surface; nymphs serving well when the fish are feeding deep down or on ascending nymphs. Upstream wet-fly fishing is a challenging but highly effective method used chiefly on rain-fed rivers, especially in the North of England. Wet flies fished across and down account for most of the sea trout caught at night.

So, why select dry-fly fishing as the tactic with which to open the second part of this book, in which we shall consider each method in turn? Certainly not because I have any particular personal preference for the dry fly, less still because I see it as being in any way better than the other methods, but for a couple of far more rational reasons.

First, it is probably the most widely used fly-fishing method, serving just as effectively on spate and limestone rivers in Scotland, Ireland, Wales and the west of England as on the chalk streams of southern and eastern England. Second, and despite the mumbo-jumbo and mystique with which late nineteenth and early twentieth century chalk-stream anglers sought to surround it, because it is actually the simplest means of catching trout and grayling, provided they are showing at least some interest in surface food. Essentially, all we have to do is select an appropriate floating fly, being guided by those we see on the water or, better still, by those we see the fish feeding on, cast it to a rising trout, and hook and land him when he takes it. The whole exercise is intensely visual and all the more rewarding for being so. But, while I shall be careful not to complicate it, there is actually a bit more to it than that.

Those who do not fish often credit anglers with great patience. Perhaps confusing patience with boredom, flyfishers almost as often deny that it has anything to do with fly-fishing, but it has. Call it stealth, caution or careful observation if you will, the consistently successful dry-flyfisher invariably spends far more time waiting and watching than actually casting. His caution starts the moment he reaches the waterside.

The surest way to make absolutely certain that you will catch nothing at all is to show yourself to the fish. Trout and grayling are extremely shy and wary creatures and they never lose their fear of man. So stealth is the keynote.

In dry-fly fishing – and, indeed, in all types of river fly-fishing apart from the across-and-down technique – start at the downstream end of the beat. By doing so, you put yourself behind your quarry, which enables you to cast upstream to him, the purpose of which will become evident in due course.

If it is necessary to walk downstream in order to reach the bottom of the beat, do so very carefully, keeping as far back from the river as possible, using any cover that may be available, keeping low and moving slowly whenever you cannot avoid passing close to the water. Having arrived at the point at which you mean to start fishing, stop and look. If you can find a tree stump (or, on a smart fishery, a low bench) sit on it. Do anything to prevent yourself from cantering back upstream, casting at random.

Watch the water. Look for flies on or above the surface and for rising fish. If you can see a fly – or, better still, a succession of similar flies – try to gauge their size and general colour and to match them with something similar from your fly box. With experience and practice, you should be able to spot and identify major hatches of duns or falls of spinners quite quickly and to select a sensible artificial almost instinctively.

If there are several insect species on the water, or if you are unable to see any natural flies at all but the fish are rising none the less, the actual manner of their rising should provide you with some guidance as to what they are likely to be feeding on.

The way in which a trout takes an item of food, inevitably displacing water and causing those familiar rings as he does so, is very largely dictated by the nature and behaviour of the food item itself. At extremes on the scale, if he is feeding on ascending nymphs a foot or so down, all the angler is likely to see on the surface is a slight bulge; in contrast, if he is taking big, active sedges, scuttling across the water in frantic attempts to get airborne, he will slash at them rather than allow them to escape.

A good deal of nonsense has been written about rise forms, especially by people seeking to show that a particular type of disturbance must inevitably show the trout to be feeding on a specific species of insect. There has long been a myth that a kidney-shaped whorl is symptomatic of a rise to the blue-winged olive and, more recently, it has been quite categorically stated that a head-and-tail rise is almost always the hallmark of fish feeding on midge pupae. 'Always' is as dangerous a word as 'never' when writing about fishing. There are too many variables – the speed of the current and the strength of the wind among them – ever to be dogmatic on this subject. But it is certainly possible to identify perhaps five entirely different types of rise form and to use them to make an intelligent guess about the kind of food the fish are most likely to be feeding on.

The Bulge

Whether they are scooping up snails, shrimps or sedge larvae from the river bed, or working back and forth in pursuit of nymphs in and around weed beds, trout moving beneath the surface cause displacement of water. If the water is shallow enough, or if the trout is not far down, the displacement will reach the surface and may be visible to the angler. At its most subtle, it may amount to nothing more than a slight rocking of a mirror-like surface; at its most obvious, it may be seen as a strong bulge or swirl. In between these extremes, the stunning of a small patch of slow-moving, wind-rippled water, or the localized disruption of the natural and obvious flow of the current, can reveal the whereabouts of a fish feeding beneath the surface.

It is intriguing to watch fish behaving thus. Trout twisting on to their sides in order to scoop shrimps and snails from the gravel on the river bed have to use upward thrusts with their tails in order to push themselves downwards and forwards. In flat water less than about three feet deep, these thrusts can force quite a sizeable bulge to the surface, usually several feet downstream of where the fish is feeding.

Bottom-feeding trout and grayling will rarely rise in the water to take something drifting above them. You are likely therefore to need quite a heavy artificial if you are to tempt them – a heavily weighted Gold-Head Hare's Ear, for example, a shrimp pattern, or one of the Czech Mate patterns that are suggestive of both shrimps and caddis pupae.

Trout taking nymphs in mid water may move sideways as much as three feet in order to intercept their quarry. They do this by turning their bodies across the stream and then giving themselves a push, turning quite gently back to head up into the stream and then sidling quietly back to their lies. It is the initial push that may create a surge of water strong enough to show at the surface, so the bulge will almost always indicate the position of the trout's lie rather than the point at which he takes the nymph. This fact assumes particular significance when fishing a nymph rather than a dry fly. Very rarely can a trout feeding on sub-aquatic food forms be tempted to take a floating artificial. By far the best medicine for them is a lightly weighted nymph such as Sawyer's Pheasant Tail Nymph, the B-WO Nymph or the Grey Goose Nymph.

The Head-and-Tail Rise

Unlike the bulge, the head-and-tail rise is one of the most obvious and identifiable rise forms on the river – and, to the beginner at least, potentially one of the most deceptive. That slow, lazy, languid porpoising, a head, a back and a tail appearing and disappearing in majestic succession, and gentle rings ebbing silently away on the current.

Think about it. It is, in fact, the unhurried action of a confident fish, a fish moving to take creatures that cannot escape, such as midge pupae, the nymphs of up-winged flies preparing to hatch just beneath the surface, duns in the process of hatching, duns that have failed to escape from their nymphal shucks, drowned spinners or adult midges. Trout thus engaged can be some of the most persistent and consistent feeders in the river. They seem to get into an almost unbreakable rhythm. They can also be just as difficult to tempt with a dry fly as bulging fish can. But they are perfect candidates for the 'damp' fly – a CDC Hare's Ear, a Klinkhammer, a Hawthorn Fly (in late May or early June), or even a Buzzer, fished right in the surface film or immediately below it.

The Surface Rise

The surface rise is probably the most familiar of all, the one we hope and expect to see as we approach the river. It is faster than the head-and-tail and causes more disturbance, and it is almost always accompanied by a 'glop', the sound of a fish breaking the surface in order to take an insect floating on it. The surface rise is the classic rise of fish taking up-winged duns floating along, waiting for their wings to dry so that they may fly off – or, sometimes, black gnats, reed smuts or daddy-long-legs.

You do not have to be an avid entomologist in order to select an appropriate floating fly. The key lies in matching the naturals on the water with artificials that approximate to them in terms of size, colour and shade. Between them, the variety of dry flies illustrated in the colour plates of trout and grayling flies should be more than sufficient to allow a sensible match to be made whatever the fish may be taking.

Surface-rising trout usually lie no more than a foot or so down, watching the surface ahead of them and simply angling themselves upwards and giving themselves a slight push as they spot a fly approaching. Having taken their prey, they leave their mouths open for an instant to allow it to be washed back towards their gullets and to enable the air they have inevitably taken with it to vent through their gills. This is why, as we shall see, the flyfisher must pause before striking to a take to a dry fly if he is to avoid pulling his artificial out of the trout's mouth.

The Slash

A slashing rise, often preceded by a visible bow-wave, is the hallmark of a fish taking a sizeable, escaping insect.

During the mayfly hatch,where one occurs, the trout, once they have become accustomed to the size and edibility of the insects and have realized that there is a surfeit of food available to them, can become almost playful, slashing at the duns with great ferocity. The obvious choice of pattern when this is happening is one of the many artificials designed to represent adult mayfly duns – the Shadow Mayfly and the Grey Wulff are good examples. The less obvious choice is a Crippled Suspender, to cater for the significant numbers of fish that become preoccupied with the hatching duns, rather than the winged adults, or even, for reasons unknown, with spent nymphal shucks.

At other times, and especially on summer evenings, slashing rises are almost invariably a signal to tie on a bushy, buoyant sedge pattern such as the Goddard Sedge or Walker's Red Sedge. Sedges scuttering across the surface in their efforts to get airborne present worthwhile but elusive targets, and the fish have to move quickly if they are to catch them.

The Sip

That soft and gentle, late evening rise form, one of the subtlest of all, the sip, is characterized by a brief kissing sound and a tiny swirl spiralling away, rather like the disappearance of bath water down a plug hole.

This is the classic rise to the spent spinner, the female up-winged fly, her life's work completed, lying dead or dying on the surface film. The fish, well knowing that his quarry cannot escape, is able to take his time, nosing gently upwards and sipping each exhausted fly down quietly and deliberately. Very often occurring towards dusk, when the wind has dropped and the sun is low, the sip is not always as difficult a rise to spot as might be expected, but it can be deceptive. It is astonishing how very small a rise form a very big trout can make when it is feeding thus. I have certainly been startled on more than one occasion when I have cast to what I thought to be a fish of modest proportions only to find myself quite suddenly attached to 3 pounds or so of very angry brown trout.

Fairly obviously, a Pale Olive Spinner, a Lunn's Particular or a Sherry Spinner are logical choices when fish are feeding on spinners, except during the mayfly season when a spent mayfly pattern such as Lunn's Spent Gnat is more likely to provide the answer.

So wait and watch, and try to establish what the fish are feeding on before starting to cast. Try to work out where the fish are, too – not just the obvious one rising like a metronome ten feet out from the bank thirty yards upstream of you, but the less evident ones.

The various ways in which you can improve your ability to see fish are discussed in the next chapter. Suffice it to say here that if you canter off in pursuit of one trout well ahead of you, you will almost certainly startle others lying behind him, which are very likely then to dart away upstream, alarming him as they go.

It is impossible to overemphasize the stealth and caution needed as you move up the bank, and the slowness. Beginners have a marked tendency to be sucked upstream by the sight of fish rising ahead of them, and when they fish with experienced and competent anglers they are often surprised at how long it takes to cover no more than a hundred yards or so of water properly.

I was given a graphic demonstration of this some years ago when fishing on the Kennet as a guest. My host and I arrived at the fishing hut at the same time as another member of the syndicate, a cheerful and charming man but a victim of polio, confined to a wheelchair. After a few minutes chat, he said he was happy to fish the short stretch of water close to the car park, and we headed off to beats further away. By the time we met up again for lunch, my host and I had covered a couple of hundred yards of water apiece and had each taken a brace of fish; our disabled companion had covered no more than twenty yards, had tucked two brace of nice brown trout into his creel and was packing up to go home.

When you have identified the nearest fish worth casting to and are reasonably confident that you know what it is feeding on, work your way into a position from which you can reach it, keeping low, moving slowly and using every available scrap of cover as you do so. Precisely how near you should try to get to the fish will depend upon the nature of the water and the bankside vegetation, and the extent to which you risk frightening him by approaching too close. Ten yards or so is the ideal, but you may have to get much nearer on a small burn or brook.

Your leader should have been very lightly greased to within two or three feet of the fly, but no closer, while you were putting your rod up, and all your dry flies apart from those with natural Cul de Canard in them should have been treated with floatant at home. Cul de Canard, or CDC, feathers are taken from around a duck's preening gland. In their natural, un-dyed state, they are heavily impregnated with oil, which makes them very buoyant. Dyeing tends to remove the oil, reducing their buoyancy.

Now, watch the fish again; reassure yourself that he is still unaware of your presence and study the rhythm of his rise. If he is coming up regularly, every thirty seconds, say, it will almost certainly pay to try to coincide the presentation of your artificial with a moment at which he may be expected to rise again anyway.

Instead of doing what most people do, pulling line from the reel as they work it out with a succession of false casts, pull as much line from the reel as you are likely to need and lay it out neatly on the bank so that it will not become snagged. In this way, you should be able to put the fly to the fish with no more than a couple of false casts.

There is a clear law of diminishing returns in fly-fishing, especially dry-fly fishing. The more often a fish sees your fly, the less likely he is to take it. So, it pays to place the first cast as accurately as you possibly can. You should aim to drop the fly lightly on to the water between 18 inches and 3 feet directly ahead of the fish. Any more and it will almost certainly have begun to drag by the time it reaches him; any less and he may not have time to react to it. If he does not take the fly, do not lift off and recast immediately, but allow it to drift back well behind him before doing so.

The moment your line and leader are on the water, the current will take hold of them, carrying them back towards you. If you are to retain contact with your fly and to be able to strike effectively, you must start to shorten line at once. On a reasonably sedate stream or river, this is best achieved with a figure-of-eight retrieve, the line coming from the butt ring of the rod over the index finger of the rod hand, so that it may be trapped against the handle if necessary, and being bunched in the other hand. In faster water, it may be necessary to strip line back over the rod-hand index finger quite quickly or, if you are using a longish rod, simply to pull line down with the non-rod hand and to raise the rod tip as the fly comes towards you.

If the fish refuses your offering, do not give up and go charging off to find another, probably no more amenable than the first. Trout, particularly brown trout, are contrary creatures and may take an artificial at the tenth, twentieth or even thirtieth presentation, although the odds against their doing so undoubtedly increase with each successive try.

It pays to rest quite frequently, watching again carefully to establish whether the original diagnoses of the fly on the water and the fish's rise form were correct, perhaps changing to a different pattern, either an alternative representation of the natural you believe him to be taking or a smaller version of the one you have been using. It is surprising how often stepping down a couple of hook sizes will elicit a take from a previously wholly uninterested trout. Occasionally, a fish will come up beneath the fly and drift back on the current scrutinizing it closely, with it almost balanced on his nose, eventually gliding nonchalantly back to his lie. When this happens, a reduction in fly size will very often provide the solution. Only when you are wholly convinced that you have put the fish down with your casting or that no pattern in your fly box has any chance of tempting him should you consider moving on, as cautiously as ever, to lay siege to your next fish.

Drag

One of the commonest causes of a trout's refusal to co-operate in running water is drag – the unnatural, cross-current movement of the artificial on the water, caused by differences in the rate of flow at various points across the stream and by the effect of those variations on line and leader. Drag may be very obvious, with the fly skidding across the surface at great speed, or it may be imperceptible. At either extreme, and at all points in between, trout hate it, and they will rarely have anything to do with a dragging dry fly.

Drag can be avoided in several ways. The first is to position yourself as nearly directly behind the fish as possible, casting straight up across his back, but this method has a slight drawback in that the leader will drop on to the water immediately above and in front of the trout and may frighten it. A more effective technique is to cast from an angle with a slack or wavy line. This is not difficult to achieve. The trick is simply to check the line just before it drops on to the water, which pulls it back very slightly towards you. In most circumstances, this should enable the fly to drift down undisturbed while the current takes up the slack in the line. In faster water, it may be necessary to mend line, that is flick it into an upstream curve as soon as it has landed, and mend it again as often as may be necessary. The problem with mending line is that it tends to skid the fly sideways across the current each time you do it, which may, of itself, pull it off course or alarm the fish.

A third option is to cast a 'shepherd's crook' – a sharp left- or right-handed curve in the leader – to avoid dropping the leader within the fish's field of view. This is quite easy to do using the technique described in Chapter 5, but it takes considerable practice to be able to put a curve into the leader and to place the fly accurately at the same time.

So you have used your best endeavours to try to catch this first fish. You are reasonably confident that you have identified what he is, or was, feeding on and that the artificial you originally chose to match it was a sensible one. You have tried a smaller version of the same pattern and, subsequently, an alternative pattern to represent the same natural, and one or two others for good measure. You are fairly sure that the fly is not dragging as it approaches the fish and, anyway, you have been casting a slightly wavy line to eliminate drag or, at least, to reduce it to a minimum. Still he has shown no interest. Indeed, he has stopped rising and appears to be sulking a foot or so beneath the surface.

Give him best. Mark his position carefully so that you may have another go at him later (there is great satisfaction to be had from eventually taking a trout that has resisted one's efforts perhaps over a number of days or even weeks) and move on cautiously to his colleague a little further upstream.

Check the new fish's behaviour carefully, once again trying to spot and identify the natural flies on the water and to analyse the trout's rise form. Check that your artificial matches the natural you believe the fish to be taking and that it is properly dry, so that it will float high and well cocked on the surface. Work yourself into a position from which you can cast to your quarry neatly and accurately, with the least risk of frightening him or allowing drag to alert him. Pull off line on to the bank and then, with just a couple of false casts, place the fly in front of him, aiming for a point 18 inches to 3 feet directly upstream of him and checking the line slightly just before it lands on the water, putting a wave into it to reduce the risk of drag. Start to retrieve with a deliberate figure-of-eight as the fly drifts down on the current.

In fast, streamy water on spate brooks and rivers, the trout's rise may be a quick, splashy affair. On more sedate, fertile waters, where surface food is borne down slowly, it is usually much more deliberate. In either case, it is intensely exciting for the flyfisher. One moment his offering is there, bobbing or drifting along on the current; the next it has gone, engulfed in a glop and a whorl, and all that is left is a circular surge of waves pulsing outwards. Instinct tells us to strike at once but, if you do so, you risk pulling the hook from your hard-earned quarry's still-open mouth.

'Oncers', Selective Fish and Fussy Fish

We all dream of prolonged, general hatches, with every fish in the river rising steadily. Such happenings are rare, and becoming rarer with the decline in chalk-stream fly life. Quite often, though, you will come across any one of three different types of rising fish. All of them can be intriguing and rewarding in their own ways. I think of them, respectively, as 'oncers', selective fish and fussy fish.

The oncer is the fish that, when there are few flies hatching and few or no other fish moving, rises just once, or just occasionally, perhaps every five minutes or so. If you know precisely where he is lying, he can often be quite an easy fish to catch. The very fact that he has risen or is rising from time to time suggests that he is in feeding mood and interested in what is going on on the water's surface. The difficulty is in knowing exactly where he is. It can be remarkably difficult to note the position of a fish that rises thirty or forty yards upstream of you and still to be certain of the position when you reach the area where you know him to be. If you do not know precisely where he is, there is a real risk that you will scare him by coming too close or by casting too far ahead of him.

The trick is to make a very careful mental note of the position of the rise, relating it to at least two clearly identifiable landmarks – two, because however obvious a landmark may seem, it is extraordinary how it can disappear as you get closer to it. Objects protruding from the water's surface such as emergent weed, reed stems, groynes and the like are more reliable landmarks than bankside vegetation.

As you approach the oncer's position, stop short of it and watch carefully. If you are lucky, he may rise again. Even if he does not, it will pay to watch for a while in an attempt to work out where local geography makes it most likely he will be, or even to see him. When you are confident you know where he is, float a fly over him. If there are no natural flies on the water, I would be inclined to start with a generic pattern, something like a CDC Hare's Ear. If that is ignored, it may pay to go straight to an eye-catching artificial such as a Daddy Longlegs. The chances are that if you can drift the fly over the fish without alarming him, he will come up and take it.

Selective fish are those that are picking out one particular species of fly or one particular phase in the fly's life cycle from among flotillas of flies, which may be far more obvious to the human eye. The classic example is the fish picking out medium olive duns, and only medium olive duns, during a respectable hatch of mayflies. One of the more bizarre examples of selectivity I have seen, and it is by no means unusual, is the fish that will gorge itself on empty mayfly nymphal shucks during a mayfly hatch. Although this seems to defy reason – there cannot be much nutritional value left in a shuck once the dun has hatched from it – it is probably because there is plenty of food about and the shucks are particularly easy to take. No less strange is a story told to me by Phil White, a hugely experienced river keeper and flyfisher, of trout during a fall of mayfly spinners becoming wholly preoccupied with half-spent insects, those that, having laid their eggs, lie on the surface for a while with one wing flat on the surface and the other up in the air.

Obvious as the answer to the selective fish may seem, it is astonishing how often people ignore it. If a fish repeatedly refuses the fly you are using as a representation of the most obvious naturals on the water, do not go on hammering away at it but stop and watch both the fish and the water's surface very carefully. Even if you do not actually see that it is taking, its rise form may give you a clue to whether it is taking emergers rather than hatched duns, for example. You may also become aware of occasional medium olives, iron blue duns or other naturals drifting down among greater numbers of more obvious flies.

Even if you cannot work out precisely what the fish is taking, it can often pay to change to a different and smaller pattern if it repeatedly refuses your first choice.

Fussy fish, as opposed to selective fish, can be both fun and frustrating. They are the fish that lie out, quite often in open water, rising frequently and regularly for long periods, even when there is no fly life of any sort to be seen on the water. They can be remarkably difficult to alarm, carrying on rising around artificials or even fly-lines, however clumsily cast. They may remain in position and continue their behaviour for weeks or even months on end, almost inevitably becoming Aunt Sallies – a fish that everyone has fished for.

For obvious reasons, such fish tend to engrave themselves on our memories. I can think of a dozen or more examples on the stretch of the Itchen I have fished for the past fifteen years or so. Some have been so taunting and tantalizing that I have even taken a pair of binoculars with me simply to try to see what they have been taking. The answer to such fish, if answer there is, and there are certainly no guarantees, seems to be to put on a tiny fly on a tiny hook – no more than a few strands of fine black fur wound on to a size 20, 22 or even 24 hook. The problem, of course, is that it can be difficult to hook fish on such small flies and, even when you do, there is always a risk of the hook pulling free.

Tightening and Playing

The length of the pause before striking will be dictated by the speed of the rise which will, in turn, be dictated in part by the type of food the fish is taking but chiefly by the speed of the current. On calm, slow-flowing rivers, and even on quiet pools on faster ones, you may have to steel yourself to observe the old rules of counting to three or saying 'God save the Queen' before lifting the rod tip. In rapid, streamy runs, you may have to tighten almost immediately.

I say 'tighten' rather than 'strike' because the word 'strike' has unnecessarily violent connotations. The action of setting the hook should be neither sharp nor violent. In fact, all that is required is to perform exactly the same movement you would use if you were going into a back cast, raising the rod and simply tightening on the fish.

Instinct impels most anglers to strike directly away from the fish. In fact, this is by no means always the most efficient way of setting the hook. If you are fishing across fairly rapid water, or if any of the line between your rod tip and the fly has drifted downstream of you, which you should have been seeking to prevent by retrieving line, it is better to strike upstream, against rather than with the pressure of the water. If you are using a fine leader point, it pays to release the line from your left hand momentarily as you strike. The friction of the rod rings on the line is usually quite sufficient to set the hook.

How a fish behaves when hooked will depend largely on the species and, to a lesser extent, on the character of the individual specimen. Brown trout tend to be strong and dogged, either heading for their chosen bolt-holes beneath a bank, among tree roots or in a weed bed, or engaging in a tug-of-war in deep water if they can reach it. Rainbow trout usually fight more spectacularly, quite often leaping from the water, but generally tiring more quickly than browns do.

If a fish is able to get downstream of the angler, both the angler and his tackle will have the weight of the current to contend with as well as the antics of the fish. This can pose quite serious problems in fast water, even with trout of only modest proportions and especially with grayling, which raise their sail-like dorsal fins and paravane back and forth across the current. It is important to keep the fish upstream of you if you can.

The line should be kept taut and the rod tip up throughout the playing of a fish. The springiness of the rod acts as a buffer, protecting the leader and the hook-hold in the fish's mouth from sudden fierce tugs and rushes. If the fish starts to pull the rod inexorably downwards, keep the tip up by allowing him to take line out; line thus released can always be retrieved later. If the fish leaps, lower the rod tip momentarily to prevent the fish from smashing the leader if he falls back on to it, and tighten again as soon as he is back in the water.

Whether you play a fish from the reel or simply by retrieving line through the rod rings and allowing it to fall on to the bank or into the water beside you is largely a matter for personal choice. There are arguments for and against both methods.

To play a fish from the reel is neat and tidy, and obviates the risk of treading on the line or having it snag on a thistle or a piece of tree root. But too many fish are lost by flyfishers being more concerned to get the line on to the reel as soon as a fish has been hooked than with concentrating on what the fish itself is doing. Also the inertia of a fly reel can be sufficient to break the leader if an unusually large or active fish makes an unexpected lunge for freedom. On the other hand, line lying loose on the ground can easily be stepped on, tangle, or become caught around an obstruction, which can also cause breakage if the fish suddenly takes off.

Whether you choose to play the fish from the reel or by hand, your objective should be to keep him clear of hazards and to bring him to the net as quickly and efficiently as reasonably possible. Trout can be steered away from obstructions by the use of side strain – tipping the rod over until it is almost horizontal and thus applying lateral pressure. If a fish does bury itself in weed, light pressure will often extricate him. If this fails, try pointing the rod directly at him and then gently hand-lining him out. Incidentally, a fish thus extracted and blinded by a swathe of weed around his head will usually come to the net wholly inert, with no further fight at all, but this always seems to me to be rather a sad end to a sporting encounter.

Throughout the playing of a fish, the angler should keep low and use such cover as may be available, not only to avoid agitating the fish he has hooked but, just as important, to avoid alarming others he may wish to pursue once this one is safely on the bank. It is quite remarkable how very much more fiercely a trout will fight if he can see the angler and his net than if he cannot.

Catch-and-Release or a Few for the Pot

The debate surrounding the relative merits of releasing fish or killing them is a complex one, arousing strong feelings. In simplest terms, it is important to recognize catch-and-release as a fisheries management tool rather than simply as a way of avoiding having to stop fishing when one has caught one's limit.

Catch-and-release is essential where a fishery sustains a healthy population of wild trout or where the owner is taking a range of measures to develop such a population. But, especially in the most populous parts of the country, the fishing pressure on some waters is so great that the demands placed on them could not possibly be met by a wild trout population alone. On such waters, the wild trout population is augmented with stocked, farm-reared fish – in some cases to the extent that the stocked fish have supplanted the wild ones.

For reasons that are not fully understood, while brown trout stocked into rivers may thrive through the spring, summer and autumn, they tend to do far less well than wild fish during the winter, a surprising number of them failing to survive their first one in the river. This being so, the owners of many stocked fisheries encourage anglers to kill the fish they catch or even insist on their doing so, limiting the number of fish an angler may take.

There is no more to be said for returning stocked fish when the fishery owner or manager has made clear that he wishes them to be killed than there is for killing wild trout on fisheries designated as catch-and-release.

Based on the fishery rules and the fishery owner or manager's views on the matter, the decision about whether to release or kill the fish caught should be taken before starting to fish, because it will affect the choice of leader and fly.

If fish are to be released, barbless hooks, or at least hooks with the barbs squeezed down, are essential. Those who are unfamiliar with barbless hooks sometimes speculate about the risk of losing fish through their use. I am absolutely convinced that I lose no more fish with barbless hooks than I do with barbed ones – and even if the odd one does come off, how much does that really matter when set against the ease with which barbless hooks allow fish to be released? People also suggest occasionally that barbless hooks wear larger holes in fishes' mouths than barbed ones. Personally, I have never seen any evidence of that. Again, I would far sooner my hooks wore away a bit of skin but came out cleanly than that they tear the flesh when they are removed, barb and all.

The faster a fish is played and brought to the water's edge, the sooner it can be released and the more likely it will be to make a rapid recovery. With this in mind, it makes sense to use a slightly stronger tippet than you might otherwise select.

If at all possible, the fish should be released in the water. I am not a great fan of the gadgets that are available for releasing fish; they seem both fiddly and unnecessary. Simply run your hand down the leader and tweak the hook free. If the shank of the hook is inaccessible, snick it out with a pair of artery forceps rather than force finger and thumb into the fish's mouth.

In the rare but unfortunate event that the hook is in the fish's gullet, it is better to cut the tippet off as short as possible and release the fish with the hook in place than to mess around trying to get it out.

If a fish brought to hand is still flapping about too much to be unhooked cleanly, it is better to net it than to engage in a splashy scuffle around one's feet. The fish should be kept submerged within the net and then released quickly and cleanly, ideally without being touched.

If it is impossible to unhook the fish in the water, perhaps because of the height of the bank or the density of the bankside vegetation, it should be netted, using a well-wetted landing net with a knotless mesh. The hook should be removed without touching the fish, and the fish should be returned to the water in the net and tipped free. It should, of course, be kept out of the water for as short a time as possible. Research conducted in Canada has shown that thirty seconds exposure to the air reduces a salmon's probability of survival by 50 per cent. There is no obvious reason why trout should be any different.

If it is absolutely essential to handle a fish – and photographing it is most certainly not an acceptable excuse – the hands should be well wetted first and the fish cradled gently on its back. For some reason, this almost always stops it struggling, enabling the hook to be extracted more quickly and with less trauma.

If a trout has been played quickly and released with the least possible trauma, it will probably dart off as soon as it is free. If it seems reluctant to do so, it should be cradled loosely in one's hands, facing upstream into a brisk flow of clean water until it is able to swim off. Under no circumstances should any part of a fish's body be squeezed or gripped tightly, which can cause serious damage to internal organs.

Released fish usually head for cover or for deep water. It is worth watching them for a few moments to be as sure as one can be that they really have recovered. If they seem unnaturally inert, or if they settle into silt or mud, a very gentle nudge with the rod tip will generally bring them round.

If a trout is to be killed for the table, wait until he is fully played out, place the net in the water, keep the rod tip up and draw him over the net. Never scoop at the fish with the net; to do so is an almost certain recipe for disaster as it will cause him to panic and bolt off again and you may well break the leader or pull the hook out in the process. If the fish is of modest proportions, he can simply be lifted from the water; if he is larger and there is any risk of his weight damaging the arms or frame of the landing net, it may be necessary to shorten your grip on the handle or even, in an extreme case, to drag it up the bank.

Once you have him ashore, the fish should be dispatched at once, as quickly and humanely as possible. Before removing him from the net or extracting the fly from his mouth, grasp him firmly across his back just behind the gills – the net will help you to obtain a secure grip – hold him upright and give him three or four sharp taps on the top of his head, immediately behind his eyes, being careful not to hit your thumb at the same time – a painful experience! Properly done, this will kill him instantly, although his nerves may make him continue to twitch or flap for few minutes. Now you can remove the fish from the net, free the hook and admire your catch.

If you are wading – a subject we shall consider in some detail in Chapter 9 – it is almost certainly better to secure the fish by hand rather than try to net him. This is easily done. When he is played out, and assuming that you do not mean to release him, draw him towards you and grasp him firmly across his back, immediately behind his gills.

When you have a firm grip, tuck your rod under one arm or, better still, trap it under a short (1½ inch) velcro- or press-stud-fastened strap sewn on to the chest of your fishing waistcoat, leaving both hands free to dispatch the fish and remove the hook. Trout killed for the table while wading can be kept in a net – not a plastic bag, which will discolour them – or on a stringer slung from your belt. A stringer is a length of cord that is passed in through one gill cover and out through the fish's mouth.

Once you have released or dispatched your quarry, you should dry your fly thoroughly and tidy it up. A fly dried by squeezing it in a folded piece of amadou and then shaking it vigorously in a tub of floatant powder can usually be made almost as good as new. Check that the hook is undamaged and that the fly is securely tied to the leader before starting to fish again.

And that, briefly, is the essence of dry-fly fishing. As the angler gains in experience, he or she will learn some of the variations on the theme that make it the intriguing and exciting sport it is. The biggest and wiliest trout in any stream or river will almost always be in the most inaccessible places, under low bridges, tucked in beneath overhanging bushes, at the bottom of the deepest, darkest pools, or in virtually unreachable back-eddies. The fish may well be feeding on something other than the most prolific and obvious species of fly on the water; who has not cursed trout picking out olives from among an armada of mayflies drifting down on the current? The evening rise can boost enthusiasm and confidence to quite unreasonable heights and, at the same time, provide some of the most rarefied frustration imaginable. The moment we begin to believe we have found the answers to particular problems, new problems will appear to bemuse and confuse. These are some of the things that make fly-fishing so intriguing.

8   The Upstream Nymph

In many ways, nymph fishing is the most challenging form of fly-fishing on streams and rivers. It calls for the ability to read the water, to work out where unseen fish are likely to be and, in clear water, to spot the fish themselves. It calls for fine judgement and accurate casting if the nymph is to be placed so that it will have sunk to the fish's feeding depth just as it reaches the fish. It calls for keen eyesight and a high level of concentration if takes are to be spotted, and it calls for quick reactions if the hook is to be set before the fish has time to spit it out.

Finding Fish

The most essential new skill needed by those who would progress from the dry fly to the nymph is the ability to see into the water – to see fish and to identify takes when they occur. Fortunately, this is not a God-given talent but a skill that we can teach ourselves, which can be developed and refined.

The first thing to do is to give your eyes as much physical help as you can. An eye-shade or a broad-brimmed hat will cut out extraneous light, and a good pair of polaroid sunglasses will reduce glare from the water's surface to a minimum. Both of these aids are essential for successful nymph fishing on clear-water streams. Having acquired them, you must learn where to look and what to look for.

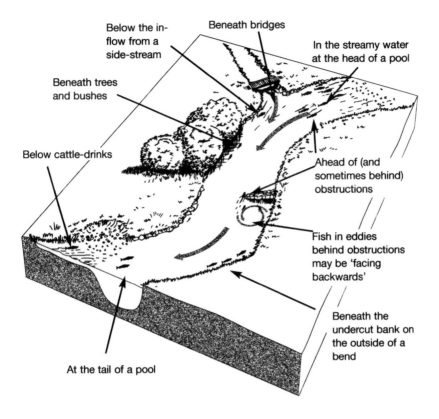

Below the in-
flow from a
side-stream

Beneath bridges

In the streamy water
at the head of a pool

Beneath trees
and bushes

Below cattle-drinks

Ahead of (and
sometimes behind)
obstructions

Fish in eddies
behind obstructions
may be 'facing
backwards'

Beneath the
undercut bank on
the outside of a
bend

At the tail of a pool

Fig. 17 Where fish lie in a river

As we saw in Chapter 2, trout seek lies that provide them with cover and protect them from the full force of the current but still allow them to take advantage of food borne down on the stream. Obstructions in a river – weed beds, weirs, groynes, bridge piles, fallen trees and branches, boulders, and so on – have areas of slack water immediately above and below them, the one at the upstream end being caused by the buffer effect of the obstruction and often quite deep, the one at the downstream end being sheltered by the obstruction and frequently quite shallow. Trout take full advantage of these slack-water areas but are far more likely to be found in the upstream buffer zones than in the downstream back-eddies.

They will also often lie in channels between weed beds, through which food will be funnelled towards them and from which they can slip into the weed itself when danger threatens or when they need respite from the current.

A string of trout is frequently to be found tight in against steep or undercut banks on the outsides of bends. Although the current is more powerful on the outside of a bend than on the inside, a steep bank produces drag which slows the stream a little, so the fish can lie in protected positions in narrow stretches of relatively quiet water and still gain access to the conveyor belt of food coming round the corner towards them. Such outside of the bend fish tend to move only very short distances to intercept food, and to rise markedly more quickly than do their brethren lying in more placid areas, because of the speed at which insects are swept past them. It is worth remembering that when you are casting to trout in such lies, your fly or nymph must be drifted round hard up against the bank, and you will probably have to strike a little faster than you would expect to have to elsewhere on the river.

Although they rarely do so at other times in the year, trout will often take up lies in hollows or depressions in broad, gravelly flats in spring and early summer when their feeding urge is at its strongest, and they may return to them in September. Perhaps surprisingly, because they are out in the open, such fish tend to be particularly well camouflaged and can be among the most difficult to spot.

Trout, often very big trout, greatly appreciate the shade and protection afforded by bridges and overhanging trees and bushes, and welcome as a bonus the various terrestrial creatures that are likely to fall into the water in such places. Lies like these can present the angler with severe problems of access and presentation, but it is well worth devoting time and effort to them.

The point at which two streams converge will almost always provide a haven for a few fish, as will the small back-eddy bays found where culverts or ditches run into a stream or river.

Lastly, areas immediately downstream of cattle drinks, where cows and bullocks stir up the bottom, dislodging shrimps, nymphs and sedge larvae to be washed helplessly away, will very often hold some of the most opportunistic – and therefore some of the largest – trout in the river. As an aside, I have no reason to disbelieve the story of the experienced flyfisher who used to wade into the water at a cattle drink holding on to a cow's tail, using the animal to provide cover from which to cast to fish feeding downstream.

Having established the sorts of places in which trout may be expected to lie we must establish what it is we are looking for. Trout and, to a lesser extent, grayling have an astonishing ability to blend with their backgrounds and can be remarkably difficult to see, especially against a background of gravel or when they are lying close to weed. The keys to spotting them are to learn to look through the water rather than at it, and to look for indications of fish rather than for the fish themselves, which will by no means always be seen as complete entities.

Exactly as they were with dry-fly fishing, patience and slowness of movement are the keys to seeing trout and thus to successful nymph fishing. Those who charge up the river banks may see a few fish – dashing off upstream in panic or scurrying for cover among the weed. But they will see none they can cast to with any expectation of success.

To start with, when you have worked yourself into a position by a pool or run where the light and the background reflected from the water's surface give you the best view into it, you may believe it to be devoid of life altogether. But as you watch very carefully you should start to see some of the telltale signs that will show you where the trout are – the upright trailing edge of a tail fin in an otherwise horizontally aligned world; a fishy shadow on the stream bed on a bright, sunny day; pale scrape marks where trout have brushed the gravel for prolonged periods with their tails; a bronze or silver flash deep down in a pool; a glimpse of white as a mouth opens and shuts on a nymph; or movement, the biggest give-away of all.

A fish that sidles into a weed bed as you approach may regain its confidence and slip back out into its lie. Another, otherwise invisible under a bush or beneath an overhanging bank, may show itself as it pushes across the current briefly to intercept an item of food and return to its cover. But most significant of all will be those that just material-ize, having been there all the time. At one moment you are peering through the water at an apparently featureless stretch of gravel, then there seems to be something strange about it, just a hint of movement – perhaps a tail waving gently, out of synchronization with the weed near it – and the next moment there is a trout, vague and indistinct, but unquestionably a trout, breasting the current.

Having located a fish, the next decision to take is what nymph pattern to present to it, and how. The former question is more easily resolved than the latter.

Nymph Selection and Presentation

Although it may be necessary to present a fair representation of the natural fly in terms of size, shape and colour when dry-fly fishing, we can really meet all of our nymphing requirements with no more than about half a dozen patterns. Pheasant Tail and Blue-Winged Olive nymphs will cater for almost all the up-winged species. A Gold-Head Hare's Ear and a leaded shrimp pattern or a Killer Bug can be useful for faster or deeper water or for fish in positions to which the artificial must sink very quickly, immediately downstream of an obstruction, for example. A black or very dark olive buzzer pattern in sizes 14 to 18 is essential on most streams, particularly in the evenings.

In addition, there are some interesting patterns with which it can be fun to experiment, especially the Czech Mate and Polish Woven nymph series, all of which are rather similar, offering remarkably real-istic representations of caddis larvae and stonefly nymphs.

If nymph selection is relatively easy, the problem of presentation is markedly less so. When dry-fly fishing, we only have to place the fly accurately in two dimensions. In nymph fishing, we must work in three, seeking to put the artificial to the fish at the right depth as well as in the right place. To this end, the nymph fisherman generally casts upstream to fish, as he would with a dry fly, placing his artificial far enough ahead of his quarry for it to have sunk to the fish's depth by the time it reaches the fish.

In theory, the problem of computing the distance required for a nymph of uncertain weight to sink to a specific depth when attached to a leader of uncertain density and cast into a current of uncertain speed may seem wholly insoluble – especially when you can very rarely see the nymph or even be sure where it is once it has disappeared beneath the surface. In reality, it is remarkable how quickly one becomes quite adept at it with a little practice.

In water of moderate pace, a size 12 or 14 Pheasant Tail or Grey Goose nymph sinks about a foot for every 4 or 5 feet travelled; a size 14 Killer Bug weighted with copper wire may sink 18 inches or so over the same distance, and a heavily weighted pattern such as the Depth Charge Pheasant Tail nymph may go down as much as 2½ or 3 feet over the same 4 or 5 feet. Of course, 'moderate pace' is a relative phrase, and much will depend upon the weight of the hook the fly is tied on, and the amount of weight that has been incorporated into the dressing. But these rules of thumb should provide some idea of how far upstream of a fish you must cast in order that the fly may reach the quarry at the right depth.

This computation of depth is important. In the previous chapter, I said that fish feeding on nymphs will rarely rise to take dry flies. Similarly, they rarely lift much above the level at which they are feeding to take nymphs, although a trout lying a foot above the bottom may sometimes go down to take a food item, or an artificial, trundling towards him along the stream or river bed.

Where the fishery rules allow more than one fly to be fished at a time, it can be worth fishing two or even three nymphs on a leader, about 20 inches apart and with the heaviest one on the point to enable the leader to turn over properly. The droppers should be formed with three-turn water knots, the upward-facing loose end being snipped off short, the fly being tied to the downward-facing one.

Detecting the Take

So we have located a nymphing fish, selected a pattern with which we believe we may secure his downfall and decided where we must put it in order that it may sink to his depth by the time it reaches him. The next problem is to identify the precise moment at which he takes it so that we may hook him.

Many flyfishers seem unable to decide whether to watch the leader for signs of a take or whether to watch the fish. I have no doubt whatever that it pays to watch the fish, and the fish alone, if you can see him, and only to resort to watching the leader when the water is turbid or severely rippled, or when glare from the surface makes it difficult to see, or overhanging bushes obstruct your view. The greatest mistake is to vacillate between the two, glancing from one to the other and, in all probability, failing to spot and correctly interpret the usually very subtle telltale signs provided by either.

When you believe your nymph to be close to the fish, if he rises or falls a little in the water or pushes to one side or the other, or if you see the white of his mouth opening or closing, tighten, and tighten quickly. The pause before striking to a rise to a dry fly has no place in nymph fishing. A trout can take and reject an artificial nymph in an instant, and you cannot strike too fast. If you are fishing with a fine point to your leader – say, 3 pounds or less – it may be worth momentarily releasing the line with your left hand as you lift the rod tip or flick it out to one side. The friction of the rod rings on the line will be quite sufficient to set the hook; if you hold on to the line, there is a risk of breaking the leader.

Should the fish fail to take your nymph as it passes him, do not be in too great a hurry to lift it from the water and recast. It is remarkable how often a trout will appear to take no notice of a nymph at all as it approaches him or when it reaches him, but then spin round and follow it downstream for some distance before actually taking it.

A useful way of improving take detection is to place the nymph so that it will drift down about a foot to the right or left of a visible fish. In order to take the artificial, the fish must swing across the current, usually straightening up as soon as it has the fly in its mouth, at which instant a strike will very often be rewarded with a satisfyingly bent rod.

Another means on water where the fish cannot so easily be seen is to use a longer rod than normal – perhaps one of about 10 feet – to cast a relatively short line and to retrieve it simply by raising the rod as the nymph or nymphs drift back towards you. Fish taking nymphs presented in this way will frequently hook themselves. Even if they do not, any sudden straightening of the line's curve is likely to indicate a take, assuming the flies are not snagging on weed, the river bed or other obstructions. As a bonus, the line can simply be left to drift back into a bow behind the angler's shoulder, enabling him to lift it into the air with a roll cast, make one false cast and then re-place it accurately on the water ahead of him.

With nymphs, as with dry flies, trout usually find drag offputting, and you should aim to allow your artificial to drift down inert on the current, which is why we cast nymphs upstream and allow them to be carried back towards us. But the induced take tactic, developed by Frank Sawyer, can be deadly on occasions, both in persuading trout to take the offerings and as an aid to hooking fish even when we cannot see them.

There is nothing complicated or difficult about inducing a take. The nymph is simply cast upstream of the fish as usual, and, as it approaches him, the rod tip is raised slightly, lifting the nymph up through the water. Whether fish believe nymphs behaving thus to be ascending to the surface to hatch or simply to be escaping, we shall never know. What is certain, though, is that they often find such behaviour irresistible, grabbing the offering determinedly and frequently hooking themselves in the process.

Coloured Water

So far we have only considered nymph fishing (and, indeed, dry-fly fishing) on clear-water streams, but this is not to suggest that either method cannot be highly effective on less limpid ones. Where any stream or river is heavily coloured with run-off water from the land, it is likely to prove unfishable. But peat-stained water, ranging in tint from light whisky to translucent slate grey, should be no less productive than a clear-water stream. Such opacity certainly makes fish location more difficult, but the problem can largely be solved by developing an ability to read the water, and at least we have the advantage that the fish are less likely to see us – although that does not argue for our being any less cautious than we would be on clearer waters.

When nymph fishing on coloured streams or rivers, you will generally be fishing the water, casting to likely lies, rather than to specific, seen, fish. While you may occasionally see a bulge in the water or a flash of bronze as a trout moves to an artificial, the surest way of detecting takes is to use a weighted nymph and to grease the top two thirds of the leader, watching it carefully as it drifts down towards you. If it checks or pulls forward, if it twitches off to one side, or if it suddenly seems to stop sinking when you expect it to continue to do so, strike, without pausing to wonder whether its change in behaviour has been caused by a fish or not.

This technique can also be used to good effect on clear-water streams, when light reflected from the surface prevents you from seeing the fish, or when he is hidden by some other obstruction.

The induced take can also be useful when nymph fishing in coloured water, the rod being raised as the nymph drifts down past a likely lie, and offers the advantages that the take tends to be felt, rather than seen, and that the fish may well hook himself.

Non-anglers and those who have not fished a nymph sometimes marvel at the sixth sense that nymph fishers seem to display – it often appears to be an almost psychic ability to detect takes and to hook fish. In truth, there is no magic involved. Concentration and careful observation are the keys to success and, with practice and experience, the nymph fisher's eyes and mind can become remarkably finely tuned to the subtlest movement in the water and to the slightest change in the leader's behaviour. Nymph fishing may, indeed, be the most testing form of fly-fishing, but it can also be one of the most effective and rewarding.

9   Wet-Fly Fishing

Dry-fly and nymph fishing can be effective on streams and rivers throughout Britain, but it takes two further techniques – wet-fly fishing, both upstream and across-and-down – to complete the picture.

Wet-fly fishing is as old as fly-fishing itself, but its development as a specialized technique only really seems to have begun during the late eighteenth century, and it was not until W.C. Stewart's book *The Practical Angler* was published in 1857, followed in 1885 by T.E. Pritt's *Yorkshire Trout Flies*, (re-titled *North Country Flies* the following year) that what is termed the north country wet-fly style was formally encapsulated in print. Since then, the technique has spread to most British river systems apart from those upon which fishery rules allow only dry-fly and nymph fishing, chiefly the chalk and limestone streams of southern England. Indeed, so widespread has it become that it could more appropriately and descriptively be termed upstream wet-fly fishing.

Where it is widely practised – in Scotland and Wales, and in the north and west of England – experienced flyfishers tend to see upstream wet-fly fishing as an alternative to dry-fly fishing rather than as a superior craft in its own right, the truly skilful angler being able to turn his hand to either technique as occasion demands.

As a general rule, north country wet flies are tied as wingless spider patterns on small hooks with short, slender, translucent bodies and soft, sparse hackles. Far from being fancy patterns, these tiny, delicate confections are used to represent a whole range of up-winged flies, sedges and stoneflies and to suggest all the various nymphal, pupal and adult stages in those insects' life cycles. Spider patterns rely on mobility for their success – both innate mobility furnished by the materials with which they are dressed, and the mobility provided by the angler's manipulation of them in the water. The five shown under the heading Wet Flies on the first colour plate of flies are no more than a representative sample drawn from dozens of widely recognized spider patterns.

Many of the rivers on which the wet fly works well tend to be more or less peat stained. It is rarely possible, therefore, to locate non-surface-feeding fish visually, so the angler has to learn to read the water and to prospect for fish, moving faster than he would when fishing a dry fly or a nymph, casting to likely lies. Clearly, the chalk-stream guideline, which suggests that a fly should be put only to seen, feeding fish, ceases to be workable under these circumstances.

Ability to read the water is a highly refinable skill based on observation and on understanding of the fishes' behaviour. Experience and local knowledge help enormously. It is always good to be able to start fishing confident in the knowledge that there will be a decent trout in a particular run or by a particular groyne, or that there should be a couple tucked in against this undercut bank, beneath that bush or among those tree roots. But even the relative beginner or the newcomer to a particular stream or river should be able to do passably well if he uses his eyes and applies a little logic and reasoning.

In the last chapter, I considered the kinds of places in which we may expect to find fish in clear-water streams. They will adopt precisely the same sorts of lies in coloured spate rivers, and what we must learn to do is to identify those lies from the visible evidence available to us.

Some will be no less obvious in coloured water than in clear. The buffer zones and sheltered areas above and below emergent obstructions – weirs, groynes, bridge piles, fallen trees, and so on; steep banks on the outsides of bends; the shade provided by trees, bushes and bridges; the points where streams join; and the sheltered back-eddies where culverts or ditches enter streams. All of these will be as evident to those who fish coloured streams as to those who fish clear ones, and all of them are likely to provide lies for trout.

It is only non-emergent features such as boulders, hollows in a gravel bottom and some weed beds that may not be immediately apparent, but even these may be locatable in reasonably shallow water or where they themselves lie not too far beneath the surface. Watch for telltale swirls, bulges and eddies and try to work out what causes them – almost inevitably an obstruction of some sort, and obstructions of all sorts provide lies for trout.

As important as being able to work out where trout are likely to be found is being able to tell at a glance where they will not be. Stickles – those shallow, bubbling, gravelly stretches between pools – rarely hold trout of any size. They should be bypassed quickly or simply used as approach routes to the pools above them. Fish, often quite large ones, will frequently be found lying in the slack water immediately above the stickle, especially close in against the banks. For some reason best known to themselves, such trout are often particularly wary and difficult to approach, and it pays to creep up on them very carefully, keeping low and using every scrap of cover available. Putting a fly to them effectively is not always easy, either, as the line is almost inevitably picked up by the fast water at the head of the stickle as soon as it lands, dragging the fly rapidly downstream. But a little thought, care and stealth in such places will often be well rewarded.

So, although you may not be able to see the fish you will be casting to, there are usually plenty of visible clues to where you may expect to find them – and where you may not.

Wet flies may be fished singly or in teams of two or three. The beginner may find it easier to fish a single fly, minimizing the risk of tangles, but a team of flies does increase the angler's chances, especially when he is unsure of the depth at which the fish are feeding becasue the point fly can be worked deeper than the dropper or droppers. In a team of three, each fly should be about 2 feet from the next.

What most certainly offers an advantage when wet-fly fishing is a rod longer than those you would normally use for dry-fly or nymph fishing. Whether you are fishing upstream, in which case the ability to maintain contact with the fly is of paramount importance, or casting across the stream, in which case you may need to mend line quite frequently and to lift considerable lengths of line from the water, a rod of 10 feet or even more will make life much easier.

That brings us to the question of whether we should fish upstream or across the stream.

In purely mechanical terms, fishing across and down is easier than fishing upstream and it certainly allows more water to be covered. Starting at the head of a pool or run, the angler casts across the stream or slightly upstream, allowing the flies to be carried downstream on the current until the line is at an angle of about 30 degrees below him. In order to allow the flies to drift as free of drag as possible, which is essential, it may be necessary to throw an upstream mend into the line as soon as the cast has been made. The real skill in this style of fishing lies in maintaining just enough contact with the flies to be able to detect takes when they come, but not so much as to cause them to drag across the current. As the line catches on the current and begins to swing across it, as it inevitably will, the angler retrieves just as much line as he must in order to be able to cast again and repeat the process, making his way slowly downstream as he does so.

Skilful as it may be when done well, fishing across the stream does have some quite serious disadvantages. In particular, it tends to be unacceptably unselective, leading to the capture of disproportionate numbers of salmon parr and undersized juvenile trout. It also produces far more pulls and tugs than solid hookings, probably because you are striking upstream and therefore pulling the hook away from the fishes' mouths rather than into them as you are when striking from a position downstream of the quarry. This is not only unproductive, it is potentially damaging to the fishery. The more often fish are pricked, the shyer they become, eventually perhaps becoming completely uncatchable.

So, chiefly for these reasons – and although, as we shall see in the next chapter, across and down is an essential and effective means of fishing for sea trout at night – I greatly prefer the upstream style when wet-fly fishing for trout and grayling. That is not to say that you should not be conscious of the opportunism that wet-fly fishing allows for. There is no reason why, while starting from the bottom of a beat and working up it, casting ahead as you go, you should not seize chances to put flies to fish that may move directly across the river from you or downstream of you, or to likely lies that can only be covered with cross-stream or downstream casts.

The basic technique of upstream wet-fly fishing could scarcely be simpler to describe. The keys to success are to fish a short line, no more than 20 or 30 feet at most; to fish quickly, constantly moving upstream, casting to likely lies or to seen moving fish; and to keep in touch with the flies by drawing line through the rod rings while, at the same time, steadily lifting the rod.

This style of retrieve creates a bow of line from the rod tip down on to the water 8 to 10 feet beyond it. The weight of the bow should be just sufficient to draw the fly along at a speed only very slightly greater than that of the current. Apart from the fact that this style of presentation often proves almost irresistible to trout, it also almost guarantees that the angler will be closely in touch with his fly and makes hooking, if not a certainty, at least very much easier. If the fish does not take the fly, it is easy to lift off and recast to it again quickly, without false casting.

This technique may be expected to account for by far the greater part of your upstream wet-fly fishing. It is a very flexible fishing method, offering almost infinite opportunity for experimentation and innovation.

Whether you maintain just enough tension on the line to lift the fly and accelerate it slightly as it comes towards you, whether you present a fly to the fish dead drift, allowing it to sink and be carried down on the current with no imparted movement, whether you induce takes as you would with a nymph, or whether, in a slow-running stream or pool, you allow the fly or flies to sink an inch or so and then retrieve them quite quickly, as you might on a stillwater, depends entirely on the nature of the water, the mood of the fish and the types of natural flies they are feeding on. All of these techniques can be effective and, once again, the key to success lies in observation.

If there is no sign of trout feeding at the surface, or if the only sign is an occasional bulge, then we may reasonably assume, or hope, that, if they are feeding at all, it will be on nymphs near the stream or river bed or around weed beds or other underwater features. Under these circumstances, it is obviously sensible to allow artificials to sink well down, and an induced take can be as effective with a wet fly as with a nymph.

Because of their smallness and delicacy, wet flies cannot easily be weighted with lead as nymphs can, but they can be dressed on relatively heavy hooks and it is perfectly possible to wind a couple of layers of fine copper wire on to the hook shank beneath the dressing, which can help. It is also sensible to degrease the leader very carefully with a mixture of fuller's earth, detergent and glycerine, and to check the fly-line at the end of the forward cast so as to put a little slack into the leader, which will allow the fly to sink rather more readily. Even when we take all these precautions, wet flies still tend to sink fairly slowly, and it may be necessary to cast quite a long way upstream of the point at which you believe a trout to be if you are to get your pattern down to the fish's depth, especially in fast water.

When trout or grayling are taking nymphs, an induced take with a wet fly can often be very much more effective than a dead drift, not just because the imparted movement is attractive to the fish but also because the movement itself streamlines a spider pattern, drawing the soft hackle fibres down along the body of the fly, giving it a nymph-like shape. The lift can be effected either by raising the rod tip a little faster as the fly comes downstream towards you – Frank Sawyer's classic induced take – or, when fishing across the stream or diagonally downstream, simply by checking the line and allowing the pressure of the current on it to accelerate the fly and lift it in the water.

Lastly, and as a further illustration of the flexibility offered by wet-fly fishing, an entirely different technique is needed to deal with a particular type of fish – an exceptional one but one found often enough to be deserving of comment. The fish is usually moving confidently and fairly regularly in slack water or a back-eddy, often tucked in beneath a steep bank or an overhanging bush. For some reason known only to himself, neither a gentle draw nor a dead drift will interest him at all. But try casting no more than a foot or so above him and then giving two or three sharp pulls on the line, from 12 to 18 inches each, or just lift the rod tip quite quickly. It is remarkable how often he will bow-wave after the fly and grab it.

Wading

Wading may or may not be important to chalk-stream anglers, depending on the nature of the water and the rules of the fishery, but it is likely to be essential to those who fish spate rivers, particularly the larger ones. The wading angler can often get into positions from which a cast can be made to otherwise inaccessible fish, and can sometimes approach fish that might otherwise have been unapproachable. Two warnings need to be sounded. Careless wading can and does frighten fish, and especially in swollen or powerful rivers or where the river bed is rocky, muddy or contains deep holes, it can be dangerous.

For all the emphasis I have laid on stealth and caution, it is a fact that an angler standing in the water or wading slowly and deliberately seems to alarm far fewer trout than does his counterpart on the bank. No doubt his silhouette is lower and, strangely, trout do not seem to associate a static and detached pair of legs with danger. The two things that do startle them are the surge of water caused by fast or sudden movement and the crunching and clattering of clumsy footsteps.

So, if you decide to wade, do so slowly and deliberately, moving carefully and feeling for each foothold in turn. It will often pay you to ease yourself into a position from which you can reach the fish you are after and then wait for a couple of minutes to assure yourself that you have not disturbed him or, if you think you may have alerted him to your presence, to let him to forget about you and settle down again.

Avoiding alarming fish when wading is one thing, wading safely is another altogether. Each year, a small number of anglers come to grief while wading, most merely getting cold, wet and perhaps a bit shaken, and a few actually drowning. It is therefore important that every flyfisher should know, first, what he or she can and should do to reduce to a minimum the risk of overbalancing or being swept away and, second, what to do if the worst happens.

Falling in while wading can be caused by several things – slipping or stumbling on rocks or boulders, sliding down a shingle bank, catching your foot in a tree root or some other underwater obstruction, sinking into the mud or simply wading out of your depth and panicking when a wader fills with water. But the commonest cause is an accumulation of events resulting from lack of thought and foresight. I have almost done it myself.

You climb into a powerful river at a suitably shallow point and wade out, being guided downstream by the shape of the rock or gravel bar on which you find yourself standing. Fine. Now turn round and try to make your way back upstream to get ashore. The weight of the current makes progress much more difficult, the bow-wave being pushed up in front of your waders pours in over the top of them and, before you know it, you are out of control.

Wading safely is largely a matter of foresight and preparation. When in any doubt about which is the more suitable, wear chest waders rather than thigh ones. Make sure your waders have soles that will provide a safe foothold on the most unforgiving river bed you may expect to encounter and, if you come across a bottom your waders cannot cope with, don't wade. Use a wading staff in all but the gentlest and most even-bedded of rivers; it can serve both as a third leg and to feel ahead of you for holes and other hazards. Examine the water carefully before you get into it; try to work out where you will and will not be able to wade and where you will be able to get out, and how. It is always easier and safer to wade upstream and then to move back downstream towards the bank than to be drawn into wading downstream and then have to move upstream to your exit point. If you begin to suspect that you are getting into difficulties, don't just plough on in hope; stop, take stock, and work out a route to safety.

If despite these precautions you do fall in, don't panic – waders full of water are no heavier in water than empty ones are on dry land. Contrary to all the old wives' tales, they will not pull you under, although they may make it a little more difficult to swim. Don't shout out – it will expel air from your lungs that should be helping to keep you afloat. Don't worry about your rod, your wading staff, your landing net or any of your other possessions.

Roll yourself over on to your back, turn yourself so that your head is upstream and your feet are downstream, spread your arms out and use your hands as paddles, both to help keep you afloat and to guide you gradually towards the bank.

Do not try to stand up and wade ashore as soon as the water is shallow enough. As you climb out, the water in your waders will become heavier and heavier – on dry land, a pair of waders full of water is so heavy as to be almost immovable. So stay on your back until you are right in the shallows and then lift your legs up, emptying the water from your waders.

Let us hope that no reader of this book ever has to test the efficacy of these emergency measures. With a little thought and reasonable care, they should rarely if ever be called for. We should certainly not allow the distant prospect of a possible ducking to detract from the pleasure of days spent wet-fly fishing on lovely moorland streams and rivers, moving cautiously upstream, casting to likely lies, watching for that swirl or flash of gold or for a pause in the fly-line's progress as it comes back towards us, slipping back a few fit, lean, beautifully marked wild brown trout, or even creeling a brace for breakfast.

10 Fishing for Sea Trout

Sea-trout fishing is quite unlike any other form of river fly-fishing. Bridging the gap between trout and salmon fishing and done chiefly at night, it is uniquely challenging and rewarding. A sizeable sea trout fizzing around in the dark can provide the fight of a lifetime; and the occasional fish taken for the pot is likely to be as delicious as any that swims.

In From the Sea

Although a few sea trout may appear in our rivers in early to mid June, worthwhile runs do not generally start until late June or July, and the fishing is at its best from July until September, tailing off as the season closes, usually towards the end of October. Timings of sea-trout runs can vary significantly from one part of the country to another but, generally speaking, the first fish we see in any numbers are the school peal (or herling, finnock or sewin, depending on where you are). These first-run fish, weighing between ½ pound and 1½ pounds apiece, are usually present in sufficient numbers to be worth fishing for by late June, most of the larger fish running from early August onwards.

Fresh-run sea trout often carry a few sea lice just as salmon do – small, quarter-inch pear-shaped parasites. The lice fasten themselves to their hosts' flanks in saltwater, feeding on the fishes' mucus, skin and blood. In small numbers, they are effectively harmless but serve to testify to a fish's freshness, dropping off when the fish has been in

Concealment and stealth are essential to successful river fly fishing

The author playing a fish on the River Piddle in Dorset

Brian Clarke fishing the pretty little River Meon in Hampshire

The Master of the Moor: Brian Easterbrook fishing a stream on the Duchy of Cornwall's water on Dartmoor

Mark Bowler fishing the River Lyon near Loch Tay

Summer sunshine: the author fishing the Arundell Arms water on the River Tamar

Summer sunshine: the author fishing on the pretty River Lyd in Devonshire

John Goddard grayling fishing on the Upper Test

Autumn: a grayling angler fishing the Tanfield Angling Club's water on the River Ure in Yorkshire

Winter grayling fishing on the Derbyshire Wye

NYMPHS AND DRY FLIES

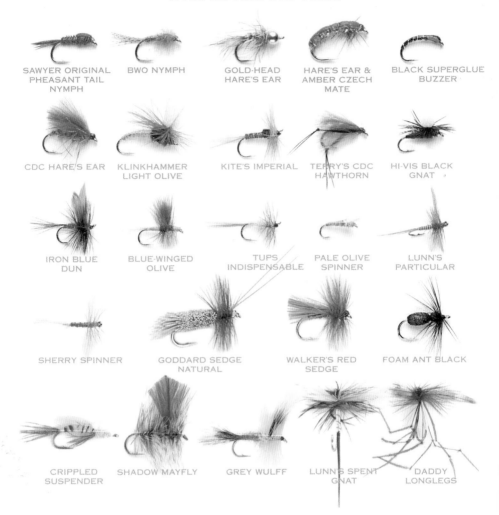

SAWYER ORIGINAL PHEASANT TAIL NYMPH

BWO NYMPH

GOLD-HEAD HARE'S EAR

HARE'S EAR & AMBER CZECH MATE

BLACK SUPERGLUE BUZZER

CDC HARE'S EAR

KLINKHAMMER LIGHT OLIVE

KITE'S IMPERIAL

TERRY'S CDC HAWTHORN

HI-VIS BLACK GNAT

IRON BLUE DUN

BLUE-WINGED OLIVE

TUPS INDISPENSABLE

PALE OLIVE SPINNER

LUNN'S PARTICULAR

SHERRY SPINNER

GODDARD SEDGE NATURAL

WALKER'S RED SEDGE

FOAM ANT BLACK

CRIPPLED SUSPENDER

SHADOW MAYFLY

GREY WULFF

LUNN'S SPENT GNAT

DADDY LONGLEGS

SPIDER PATTERNS

BLACK PENNELL

GREENWELL'S GLORY

PARTRIDGE & ORANGE

PARTRIDGE & YELLOW

SNIPE & PURPLE

SEA TROUT FLIES

ALEXANDRA BUTCHER KINGFISHER BUTCHER CONNEMARA BLACK DUNKELD

INVICTA MALLARD & CLARET PETER ROSS TEAL, BLUE & SILVER MICKEY FINN

DAVID'S BLACK BUMBLE ALLY'S SHRIMP FALKUS SUNK LURE WHITE BOMBER

GRAYLING FLIES

BEACON BEIGE CAPERER RED TAG TERRY'S TERROR TREACLE PARKIN

WITCH CJ'S TWINKLE GULPER TERRY'S EMERGER ORANGE SAWYER KILLER BUG SPECIAL KILLER BUG

SPOT-ON SHRIMP TAN GREY GOOSE NYMPH DEPTH CHARGE PHEASANT TAIL NYMPH CREAM/BROWN POLISH WOVEN NYMPH AMBER & ORANGE CZECH MATE

An autumn idyll: a grayling angler on the River Hodder in Lancashire

Fishing in Lilliput. Ted Grant fishing the Portsmouth Services Fly Fishing Association's water on the River Meon in Hampshire

freshwater for a few days. In recent years, though, dreadful damage has been done to sea-trout stocks in Scotland and Ireland by sea lice from salmon farms. Infesting seaward-bound sea trout in vast numbers, they have killed countless fish and induced many others to return to freshwater rather than migrate to sea. As a result, sea-trout runs on many previously productive rivers in Scotland and Ireland have been reduced to trickles. Elsewhere, though, in northern England, Wales and the West Country, and in Scottish and Irish rivers that are not blighted by estuarine salmon farming, sea-trout runs can be as good as they ever were, providing spectacular sport.

As the spawning urge builds in them, sea trout make their way back towards the rivers in which they were born, often idling around in the estuaries, drifting in and out on the tide, waiting for a spate. Compared with the near-flood conditions demanded by salmon, it needs only quite a modest spate to encourage sea trout to run; a day of moderate rain and a slight rise in the level of the river are usually sufficient.

Sea trout can cover considerable distances on entering freshwater. New arrivals may travel upstream for as much as seven or eight miles on their initial runs although, of course, by no means all fish move so far. Some will pause for a while in the first pool they come to, waiting for a further spate; others may cover three or four miles before resting.

Once in freshwater, sea trout can be divided into three groups – runners, resters and residents.

As their name implies, runners are fish on the move. The peal tend to travel in shoals; larger fish may move in smaller groups or individually. They move through stickles more quickly than through pools and may frequently be seen surging and slithering up through shallow, fast-running stickles, their backs right out of the water. Even where the water slackens and deepens, they will keep pushing ahead steadily. By definition, they may be found almost anywhere there is a flow of well-oxygenated water. Naturally, there are far more of them when there has been some rain.

Resters are fish that are drawing breath on their way upstream. They are frequently found lying on the shelf at the tail of a pool, often with the largest fish at the head of the shoal. If they have run a great distance and therefore need to rest for a protracted period, or if the water level becomes very low, making continuation of the run impractical or unattractive, they are likely to spread out in the pool, seeking shelter in deep water beneath steep, undercut banks or in the pads of water in front of rocks or boulders. Resters are often the shyest and most easily frightened fish but also the most catchable if approached cautiously.

It is likely to take only the slightest rise in the river to cause resters to move on again. From the angler's point of view, this is significant becasue a pool that fishes well one night will not necessarily do so the next if the fish have moved on upstream; even fish seen in a pool in daytime may no longer be there that night. Similarly, of course, a pool wholly devoid of fish one night may quite easily hold a good head the next.

Residents are fish that stay in pools for protracted periods, generally because they have reached or almost reached the areas in which they will spawn. In dry weather, though, and especially in prolonged periods of drought, a group of fish may remain in one pool for days or even weeks before running on up the river, effectively becoming resident. Resident fish can be very difficult to catch, partly because they seem to switch off and partly because they tend to work themselves into deep, dark, safe lies where it can be difficult to present flies to them.

Pools and Runs

In order to understand what follows, we need to understand the differences between pools and runs and some of their essential characteristics.

Pools are quite clearly defined. Each one has a head, where the fast water runs into it, often gouging out quite a deep hole through which the water swirls and eddies before moving on into the more sedate belly. The belly may be short or long, perhaps consisting of a series of sub-pools. If it includes a bend, the water on the inside of the bend will almost always be shallower than that on the outside, which may run beneath a steep, undercut bank. At its tail, a pool will usually shelve up quite gently before discharging its water into the next stickle or over a weir, natural or man-made. The short stretch leading up to the outflow

– often a good fish-holding area – may be known variously as the shelf or the hang.

Runs are quite long stretches of water of medium depth and are quite often rather canal-like and difficult to read.

Every pool and every run is unique, with its own geography, features and character. Inevitably, much of what follows is generalization. Unless you know a particular stretch of river really well, there is no substitute for seeking local advice from those who may willingly provide it, ghillies, fishing instructors and knowledgeable hoteliers being likely to be more helpful than local anglers.

Of Timing, Light and Weather

Few of us have the good fortune to have sea-trout fishing on our doorsteps and therefore to be able to choose precisely when we will fish. But, if happiness is the extent to which expectation is matched by reality, we can at least ensure reasonably consistent contentedness by understanding the conditions that make for good sea-trout fishing, and those that do not.

Night fishing does not mean heading for the river after dinner, fishing through the dusk and into the first hour or so of darkness and then heading for our beds. It means arriving at the water just as it is getting dark, praying for as dark a night as possible, restraining yourself from making the first cast until the very last glimmer of light has gone and then, perhaps, fishing through until first light. It is not a pastime that is likely to endear you to your spouse unless your spouse fishes as keenly as you do.

Moonlight is disastrous to sea-trout fishing. If possible, fishing trips should be planned when the moon is at its slenderest. If they cannot be, then you must hope for thick cloud cover.

Mist on the water does the sea-trout angler no favours, either. It may not kill sport completely, but it does seem to cause the fish to seek out deeper water, making it necessary to change to a sink-tip line or even a sinker in order to get flies down to them. Even then, the fish seem less inclined to take a fly than they are when the air is clear.

Reconnaissance

The prospect of night fishing may seem daunting, particularly to those unused to darkness, solitude and the almost always harmless sounds of the countryside at night (*pace* the occasional unexpected bull!). But careful preparation can greatly reduce the problems it poses.

Especially on water with which you are unfamiliar, it is essential to conduct a reconnaissance in daylight, ideally during the morning or early afternoon, so as to give the fish plenty of time to settle down again before you start fishing later on.

Approach the water very, very cautiously. Sea trout are quite extraordinarily shy, and it is all too easy to startle one, his panic spreading almost instantly to the other fish in the pool. Crawl up to the river bank using every scrap of cover available. In a clear-water stream or river, you may see the fish you will be casting to later. Especially in bright weather, some of them will probably be lying in quite close-packed shoals in relatively deep, slack water in the shade provided by overhanging banks, trees or bushes, moving very little. The majority of these fish are likely to be residents. The resters are likely to be in slightly streamier water, a little further out from the bank, and on the shelf towards the tail of the pool.

Fig. 18 Typical distribution of sea trout in a pool

Check points of access to the water for hazards or obstructions; see where you will and will not be able to wade safely; and examine the back-cast area carefully for potential snags – trees, bushes, barbed-wire fences, and so on. It is worth actually trying a few casts across the river and tying a piece of cotton tightly around your fly-line where it passes through your left hand when your fly is landing a foot or so from the far bank. This will act as a marker in the darkness and is an almost fool-proof way of casting right across a pool without risking becoming caught up in the vegetation on the far side. If you plan to fish in two or three places during the night, there is no reason why you should not put two or three markers on to the line, assuming that you can remember which one serves which fishing station.

It is important to disturb the water as little as possible during your reconnaissance. If you think it necessary to try a few casts, your exploratory visit should be conducted during the morning before your expedition, rather than in the afternoon or evening, to give the fish plenty of time to settle down again.

On most rivers, particularly when they hold plenty of fish, a single decent-sized pool should be sufficient to keep you occupied throughout the night. If the sea trout are unco-operative in the stretch of water you have chosen, it is very unlikely that they will be any more obliging elsewhere. But there is never any harm in at least taking a look at a second pool and even a third one, if only because a change of surroundings at two or three in the morning can so often restore flagging enthusiasm and confidence.

Where runs are concerned, and if expert local advice is unavailable, it makes sense to concentrate your efforts on any area offering cover to the fish – a particularly high stretch of bank or, better still, overhanging trees or bushes.

Tackle and Flies

The keys to carefree night fishing are to carry the smallest possible number of bits and pieces, to know exactly where everything is and to reduce knot tying to a minimum or, ideally, to eliminate it altogether.

Of the three possible motives for fish to take an artificial fly – hunger, curiosity and aggression – the first is by far the strongest and most consistently predictable in non-migratory trout. That is why the patterns used to catch such fish are generally representative of the creatures they eat. When we come to sea trout, it is a different story. Although they will quite often take a passable imitation of a natural fly if the opportunity presents itself, they do not habitually feed in freshwater once they have been to sea. So, many sea-trout flies are designed to arouse curiosity and aggression in the fish rather than to appeal to their appetites.

Effective fly patterns for sea trout are legion, varying enormously and apparently inexplicably from one part of the country to another – from Hugh Falkus's famous, large and sparsely dressed Sunk Lure, so deadly on northern rivers, through the more traditional size 8 to 12 Alexandras, Butchers, Dunkelds, Invictas, Peter Rosses and Black Bumbles that are so popular on streams in Wales and the south-west, to Ally's Shrimps and a series of surface patterns such as the White Bomber, which may be expected to work almost anywhere. When sea-trout fishing, it always pays to seek informed local advice about fly patterns, and to heed it, however much it may seem to be at variance with your experience on other waters.

If no local advice is available, there are two reasonably reliable rules that can be used to aid fly selection. The first is that the size of the fly should be governed by the state of the water. Immediately after a spate, when the water is still quite heavily coloured, it usually pays to fish quite a big fly – a size 8 or even a size 6. Fly size should be reduced as the water clears. In really low, clear water, it may be necessary to go down to hook sizes as small as 12 or even 14. The second rule is that the way in which a fly is fished is generally more important than the choice of fly itself, which leaves you free to pick the fly in which you have confidence.

Set up your rods at home or in your hotel. If you expect to use both a floating and a sinking or sink-tip line, it is sensible to put up two rods rather than have to fiddle around changing lines at one o'clock in the morning. Tie your first choice of floating and sinking patterns to leaders and attach the leaders to the floating and sinking lines with loop-to-loop joins (see Appendix 1). Make up spare leaders with each of your first-choice patterns on them to cater for emergencies, and with such second- and third-choice patterns as you may deem necessary, and tie large (3 inch) loops into the butts of these leaders before winding them individually around a piece of stout cardboard from which you can readily free them when they are needed.

Many sea-trout anglers fish wet flies in teams of two or three. Each fly added to the leader increases the risk of tangles, especially at night. It seems sensible, therefore, for the novice to begin with a single fly, adding a second and perhaps a third (about 2 feet apart) as experience and confidence grow.

If the water you plan to fish is not too hedged about with trees and bushes, it is better to use a long (9 foot upwards) rod than a short one. A long rod will make casting easier, give you better control over your line – enabling you to mend it more easily when necessary – simplify the playing of often very energetic fish and reduce the amount of line you have to retrieve before lifting off to recast.

Leaders for sea-trout fishing need to be very much stronger than those used for brown trout or grayling because the quarry tends to be larger, to take more fiercely and to be markedly more acrobatic when hooked. Eight-pound points are by no means too heavy, even when fishing for school peal, and it is as well to go up to 10 pounds when larger fish are likely to be encountered.

Ideally, if you have sufficient leaders made up in advance and if you know where all your tackle is, you should never need a torch when sea-trout fishing at night, but it is as well to take one just in case. By far the best are those with flexible necks, which can be clipped to a fishing jacket or waistcoat and which cast a bright but concentrated beam of light. It is a good idea to cover the head of the torch with a red filter of some sort – a piece of red cellophane or some such – because red light disrupts our night vision far less than white light.

Night Fishing

When all is ready, and as dusk is falling, head for the waterside, but do not be in too great a hurry to start fishing. If you start casting too early there is a real chance that you will alarm the fish, putting them down and spoiling your first couple of hours' sport, often the most productive ones.

So enjoy the sunset and study the water. There are few greater pleasures than to sit by an attractive river, watching and listening to the wildlife around you as the stars come out in a darkening sky. Twenty minutes or half an hour spent accustoming your eyes to the darkness is time well spent.

When darkness has fallen, you can start fishing in earnest, but do so cautiously. Start at the head of the pool, a few yards back from the water, and put out enough line to cover no more than a third to a half of the river at an angle of about 45 degrees downstream, allowing the line to swing gently round on the current until it is hanging almost directly below you before lifting off and recasting. Sea trout that may have been lying in quite tight shoals in the shade or in cover provided by steep banks in daylight will probably have spread out during the evening, and there is no point in alarming fish close to you by hurling your initial casts at the far bank. If you cast too directly across the stream, the line will usually be carried round on the current at breakneck speed, skidding the fly along just beneath the surface behind it.

I usually start with a floating line and a reasonably large (size 8) traditional wet pattern – a Butcher, a Dunkeld or perhaps a Teal & Blue, a Black Bumble or Hugh Falkus's Medicine.

As you lengthen your cast diagonally downstream towards the far bank, the need to mend line will probably increase. Your aim should be to allow the fly to sink quickly and then to work it across the current, maintaining its depth as far as possible. To this end, you should mend a floating line as soon as it hits the water, flicking an upstream curve into it, to give the fly time to sink, feel for the weight of the stream on the line and mend line again as and when necessary.

A useful alternative to mending line is to slip it – a technique I have not heard or seen described elsewhere but one that has stood me in good stead on numerous occasions and one that works as well with a sinking line as with a floater. The trick is to pull between 5 and 10 yards or so of line off the reel in addition to the amount you mean to cast.

Then, once the cast has been made, some or all of the extra line can be slipped gradually and evenly through the fingers of the non-rod hand, being pulled out by the weight of the current and serving to slow the fly's passage across the stream.

Keep the rod tip low but do not point it directly down the line. Instead, hold it at an angle to the line and use it as a shock absorber to cushion the leader against the sudden impact of an often fierce take. A sea trout's take may be felt as a gentle tug or as a ferocious, explosive yank on the line, the fish erupting from the water in a cloud of spray. Between these two extremes is the frustrating tap-tapping caused by fish plucking at the fly rather than taking it properly; possible cures are to change to a smaller fly or to speed up your retrieve.

However the take comes, get your rod tip up quickly, keep your fingers clear of the reel handle and be prepared to allow the fish to take out line, possibly all of it. Until they have hooked a few sea trout, most flyfishers wholly fail to appreciate the extraordinary power of these fish. Even a modest school peal of a pound or so can tear off downstream at astonishing speed, stripping line from the reel and turning only reluctantly at the tail of the pool – if, indeed, he does so at all – before dashing off again in whatever direction takes his fancy.

The principles of playing and landing sea trout are exactly the same as those for playing and landing brown or rainbow trout but the process is usually made tenser by the ferocity of the quarry and by the darkness. Try to keep him under control as far as you can and use as much pressure as you may within the limits imposed by your tackle to bring him to the net as quickly as possible.

When you have him to hand, either release him carefully by running your hand down the leader and tweaking out the barbless, single hook, or net or beach him, dispatch him quickly and humanely and put him somewhere safe. That nocturnal pest the feral mink is now so common and determined as to present real problems. Fishing on the Torridge at night, I have had a sea trout stolen from the bank no more than ten yards from me. The safest answer is to put your catch into a fish bass (not a plastic bag) and to hang it from the branch of a tree or from a gate or fence post.

If, after a couple of hours, I have had no response to the wet fly on the floating line, or if the fish stop taking, I usually change to a sinking or sink-tip line, replacing the leader on the floating line with one with a surface lure attached – a White Bomber or a cork– or ethafoam-bodied pattern – against the likelihood that I may wish to use it later on.

It is at this point that so many inexperienced sea-trout anglers give up and potter off to bed. They are usually doing themselves a disservice. While sport during the dog watches is not always as spectacular as it can be during the first couple of hours of darkness, it can often offer the chance of a really big fish or two. As I change from the floating line to the sinker, I sometimes move to my second-choice pool as well, both to rest the one I have been fishing and to give myself a change of scenery.

The lure should be fished close to the bottom in exactly the same way and at very much the same speed as the wet fly was, with line being slipped to control and slow the progress of the fly down and across the stream. Now, though, it will often pay to retrieve the lure until there is no more than 4 or 5 feet of line beyond the rod tip rather than simply to lift off and recast as soon as it has crossed the current. The retrieve, in staccato pulls, will quite often elicit a response from a fish that may have been wholly indifferent to a fly drawn across the stream in front of him.

If the tandem lure produces no response, the surface one may. Any reasonably large, buoyant pattern will do, but the technique for fishing it is entirely different from that used for a wet fly or a tandem lure. This time, it is the skittering commotion made by the fly's passage across the surface that attracts the fish, rather than the fly itself, so fish it quite quickly.

Instead of casting at an angle downstream, cast more directly across the pool, allowing the current to catch the line and drag the fly round, and there will usually be no need to mend or slip line. Takes to fast-fished surface lures can be the most ferocious of all, and it is important to keep the rod at an angle of at least 45 degrees to the line in order to cushion the shock.

So, tired and weary, the sea-trout angler makes his way home at first light. Those who are able to spend several successive nights sea-trout fishing during the summer tend to turn the clock on its head, sleeping through the mornings and heading off to the river as darkness falls.

Daylight Fishing

Although the majority of sea trout taken from rivers are caught at night, it would be entirely wrong to suppose that they cannot be caught in daylight. The problems, of course, are obvious and have chiefly to do with the fishes' pronounced shyness, which argues for the use of long leaders with relatively fine points, generally between 6 pounds and 8 pounds. Given the sea trout's extraordinary energy, it can pay to insert a short length of power gum between the butt of the leader and the braided loop on the fly-line to cushion the shock of a fierce take or a particularly ferocious fight.

My own experience suggests that by far the best time to fish for sea trout in daytime is when the river is clearing after a spate, especially if that spate has followed a period of dry weather. In low-water conditions, there is a strong relationship between the natural colour of the water and the relative ease with which it gives up its fish in daylight. Rivers that are naturally peat stained are usually more productive than those in which the water runs clear, and the heavier the peat stain the greater their productivity, presumably because the colour in the water helps conceal the angler's designs from his quarry.

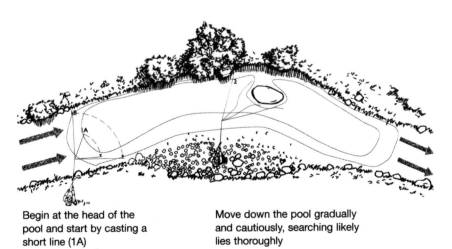

Begin at the head of the pool and start by casting a short line (1A)

Move down the pool gradually and cautiously, searching likely lies thoroughly

Fig. 19 Fishing down a pool
(The best strategy when the water is clearing after a spate)

If I have emphasized the need for stealth and caution throughout this book, I would re-emphasize it here. Sea trout are desperately nervous, edgy creatures; the first careless clump on the bank or on the river bed, the first glimpse of human movement, the first flickering of a shiny fly-line over them or the first splash of a clumsy cast will spread panic throughout the pool.

Whether one fishes down a pool or up it in daylight depends very much upon the state of the water. If it is reasonably coloured – either naturally quite heavily peat stained or only partly cleared after a spate – it can pay to fish down it as you would when fishing at night. When the water is clear, though, starting at the tail of the pool or run and working up it means that you will generally be approaching the fish from behind and thus minimizing the risk of alarming them.

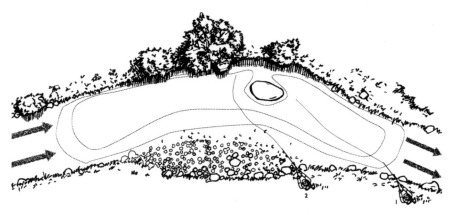

Begin at the tail of the pool, keep out of sight and fish a longish line upstream.
Move upstream gradually and very cautiously, exploring likely lies carefully.

Fig. 20 Fishing up a pool
(The best strategy in low water conditions)

With a fine, carefully degreased leader of between 12 and 16 feet and small traditional wet fly, or team of wet flies (size 12 Dunkelds and Invictas can be very effective), creep into position at the tail of the pool and cast diagonally up and across it. If the water is clear and you can see the fish, cast to those at the back of the shoal first rather than line them by casting to larger fish further up. If you elicit no interest, allow the fly to drift back well below the fish before lifting off and recasting. Just once in a while, a take-inducing lift with a wet fly will provoke a reaction in peal that seem otherwise wholly uninterested, but the reaction is as likely to be panic as a follow and a positive take, so it is probably as well to reserve this tactic for use as a last resort, when a dead drift has failed completely.

While on the subject of daytime sea-trout fishing, some mention must be made of what is, to be honest, that most esoteric of fly-fishing crafts, dry-fly fishing for sea trout. It poses a strange conundrum. Like many other people, I have caught fair numbers of sea trout – mostly peal of around a pound – while dry-fly fishing for brown trout, usually on size 14 or 16 Blue-Winged Olives and the like. Since sea trout do not feed in freshwater, and since the stomachs of the fish concerned have invariably been empty, there is no obvious reason why they should have taken such flies. Such incidents have a rarity value that makes them intriguing curiosities rather than everyday events, and the chief virtue of dry-fly fishing for sea trout is that it makes a significant contribution to the conservation of sea-trout stocks.

Fishing the Estuary

So far we have only discussed fishing for sea trout in freshwater, but there is another type of sea-trout fishing, in salt or brackish water, which is utterly different in character but certainly no less rewarding.

Sea trout in estuaries and coastal waters can be divided into two categories – those that have, as yet, no urge to return to freshwater to spawn but are simply wandering around in estuaries and along the coast, and those that are actively preparing to run up a river to spawn.

In estuaries, both types of fish tend to drift in and out with the tide, moving up towards freshwater on the rising tide and drifting back again on the ebb. It pays to be aware of this tendency. Ideally, if you can, fish near the mouth of the estuary for an hour and a half or so as the tide starts to rise; spend a couple of hours in the middle of the estuary when the tide is half way in; and then have two or three hours at the head of the estuary towards the end of the flow and at high water. Reverse the process for the ebb, spending two or three hours in the middle as the water recedes and having a final fling near the mouth during the hour before low water and for an hour or so after it.

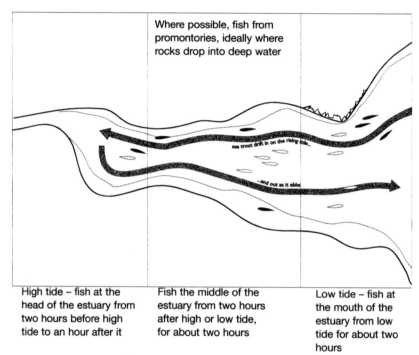

Where possible, fish from promontories, ideally where rocks drop into deep water

sea trout drift in on the rising tide

and out as it ebbs

High tide – fish at the head of the estuary from two hours before high tide to an hour after it

Fish the middle of the estuary from two hours after high or low tide, for about two hours

Low tide – fish at the mouth of the estuary from low tide for about two hours

Fig. 21 Fishing an estuary

While very little research has been done on the subject, I have the clear impression that sea trout – and certainly feeding sea trout – tend to confine themselves to relatively shallow water, perhaps up to about twenty feet deep. Rocks and seaweed provide them with both food and cover. It therefore pays the flyfisher to concentrate on such areas, but the potential penalties for doing so are obvious. Seaweed can be immensely strong. Once caught in it, or on a rock, a fly may be difficult or even impossible to free; and a sea trout taking a fly alongside a weed bed or beside jagged rocks will almost always – and very sensibly – head straight into them, often becoming very difficult to extricate.

There is a strong case for using larger flies in saltwater than in fresh and, particularly, for picking patterns that represent or suggest the creatures sea trout feed on, usually shrimps and small fish.

Perhaps surprisingly, it is by no means always necessary, or practicable, to fish deep. Indeed, one may expect at least as much success with a floating line, a sink-tip or an intermediate as with a true sinker. Flexibility is the key to success and it will often pay to experiment by fishing at various depths.

By the same token, it is sensible to vary the style of your retrieve until you find a formula the fish respond to. There seems to be no hard and fast rule for this. It could be supposed that fish-like patterns should be made to behave like fish and shrimp-like patterns like shrimps, but the reality seems to be less rational. I have caught estuarine sea trout with shrimps and streamers with slow, figure-of-eight retrieves and by stripping the fly back furiously.

Finally, and for all the difficulties I have described, the real problems with sea-trout fishing are that it is highly addictive and that it is somewhat antisocial. It is, without doubt, one of the most exciting and rewarding forms of fly-fishing. Even those who go in pursuit of salmon usually give the sea trout a higher rating, pound for pound, than their primary quarry. But it does make for lost mornings and bleary eyes, and if wives or girlfriends are not also addicted to it at an early stage, it is probably best reserved for solo or bachelor party holidays.

11   The Lady of the Stream

A by-product of the dry-fly purism that dominated the chalk valleys of southern England during the first seventy-five years of the twentieth century, and which echoes around them to this day, was the re-classification of grayling as vermin. Trout came to be seen as the only fish worthy of the true dry-fly man's attention. All other species were at best incidental and irritating; at worst pests to be eradicated.

Victorian chalk-stream anglers placed equal value on barbel, grayling, perch, pike and trout. Even Halford, founder of the dry-fly cult, acknowledged the grayling as an asset to any fishery; and beyond the chalk streams, especially in the north of England, the grayling continued to be seen as what it is, a fine sporting fish.

Over the past twenty-five years or so, growing disillusionment with dogmatic purism and with overweight and relatively easily caught stocked trout, and growing respect for truly wild fish, has done much to rehabilitate the grayling of the chalk streams. The shift in perception has been greatly helped by the excellent work the Grayling Society has done to promote the species. Today, the 'lady of the stream' is widely recognized as a worthy quarry, even the primary quarry, for many flyfishers from late summer onwards.

There is a significant difference in the practical, rather than statutory, length of the grayling seasons on chalk streams and spate rivers.

Like coarse fish, grayling spawn in the spring, and they are subject to the statutory close season for coarse fish – in England and Wales, from 15 March to 15 June inclusive. There is no close season for coarse fish in Scotland and, since there are no grayling in Ireland, the fact that there is no coarse fishing close season there, either, is academic.

Chalk streams, fed from water tables that gradually subside during the summer, are at their lowest and slowest in September and October and are usually only temporarily discoloured by rainwater running off the land. But heavy rainfall in October, November and December replenishes the aquifers, and by January the springs feeding the winterbournes will generally have broken. The streams and rivers will be strong and swollen and may well become stained as they carry away several months' worth of debris accumulated along their banks. Generally speaking, nature tends to bring the grayling season on the chalk streams to a close at the end of December or the beginning of January.

Spate rivers, having no water tables but relying instead upon rainwater draining directly off the land, do not show this gradual but sustained change in height, rate of flow and colour. Rather, they rise and fall relatively rapidly in response to showers and storms, maintaining reasonably constant mean levels throughout the year, falling below them in periods of drought and rising above them only quite briefly during and after downpours. So, where grayling thrive in spate rivers, especially in Scotland and in the north of England, it may be possible to fish for them until the end of February, by which time the fish will close the season for us as they come into spawning condition and begin to move on to their redds.

It should also be said that fly life on any river is at its least prolific and evident in mid- to late winter, and that for this reason, and because grayling tend to lie deep down in cold weather, bait fishing is usually more productive than fly-fishing from mid to late December until the end of February. I shall not be considering bait fishing in this book – not because I have any reservations about it but because I have very little experience of it, and it would be foolish to write about a subject of which I would be a far better student than a mentor.

So let us consider autumn and early winter fly-fishing for grayling, and let us hope for cold days and clear streams, for these are the conditions under which this pretty fish gives of her best.

It is a mistake to think of grayling fishing simply as a form of autumn or winter trout fishing. Although grayling may be caught accidentally when we are trout fishing, and often are, they are sufficiently different from trout in character and behaviour to warrant careful thought and specialized techniques when we set out specifically to catch them.

Finding Fish

The first problem posed for the would-be grayling angler lies in actually locating the fish. Unlike brown trout, which are intensely territorial, the grayling is a nomadic creature. Preferring water of even depth and with a steady flow in summer, she generally retreats into deeper water as the temperature drops and by midwinter will usually have settled deep into the deepest pools. She is a bottom dweller, too, almost always lying close to the river bed, which also makes location difficult, particularly when the water is dark and swollen.

Apart from a tendency to gravitate towards deeper water as the weather gets colder, the grayling's movements can be as unpredictable as the sea trout's. You may locate fish in a particular pool or run one week and find them gone the next, or convince yourself that a stretch of water is wholly devoid of life and then find it teeming with grayling a few days later.

The only help the grayling gives us lies in the fact that she is innately a gregarious fish. Individual grayling – very often the large ones – may be found lurking in deep, dark holes, tucked in beneath steep banks or hiding in inaccessible lies beneath overhanging bushes. Generally, though, medium-sized grayling congregate in shoals; if you catch one there is a fair chance that you will be able to take several more from the same place, even if you cannot see that they are there. Grayling also tend to be less shy than trout, but this does not mean that you can be clumsy in the way you approach them.

As an aside, it is interesting to compare the respective ways in which trout and grayling behave when their suspicions are aroused, perhaps by an angler on the bank. The trout will usually hold its station, sink a little in the water and become noticeably more alert and vibrant; its body seems to tense and its fins move faster, almost fluttering. A trout behaving thus will usually prove virtually uncatchable, being markedly more concerned with the suspected threat than with feeding. If its suspicions are confirmed, it will dart for cover or dash off up- or downstream. The grayling shows none of the physical tension or fin fluttering of the trout, but usually drops warily backwards if she believes that something is amiss. Having done so, she then tends to hold her new position, only turning tail and fleeing if the angler does something very obvious, such as standing up on the skyline to cast or walking on upstream along the bank. Even such wary grayling can sometimes be tempted to take an artificial fly, especially an accurately presented nymph.

Nymph Fishing

Early in what may be termed the grayling season – in late summer and early autumn – you can often fish for non-rising grayling lying in water of moderate depth just as you would for nymphing trout, and with the same patterns. The only one I would add would be Frank Sawyer's Grey Goose nymph, designed to represent the nymph of the pale watery, which can hatch in large numbers in the evenings in September and October. Where the fish are lying in deeper water, though, which is where you are increasingly likely to find them as the weather gets colder, the angler encounters another problem.

As is evidenced by their undershot lower jaws, grayling are very largely bottom feeders, probably taking as much as 90 to 95 per cent of their food – chiefly shrimps, snails, midge and sedge larvae and the nymphs of various up-winged flies – from or very close to the bottom. This poses several difficulties – getting an artificial down to the fishes' feeding depth, presenting it realistically in often fast-flowing water, and identifying takes when fishing deep down to fish you are rarely able to see.

The solution to getting patterns deep enough is to weight them heavily and to fish them on long leaders. The amount of weight required – and, indeed, the length of the leader – will depend upon the depth of the water to be fished and the force of the current. Neither should be underestimated. Too much weight and too long a leader can usually be compensated for simply by casting not quite so far upstream of the fish as you might otherwise have done. Too little weight or too short a leader offer nothing but frustration, making it quite impossible to get the fly down to the fish.

Artificials to represent most of the creatures that grayling feed on at the bottom can be tied with enough weight in them to make them sink quickly, although the nymphs of up-winged flies are rather too small and slender to be imitable with a pattern usable in runs of more than moderate depth.

Several excellent quick-sinking patterns have been devised for deep-water grayling fishing. The longest established of them is Frank Sawyer's Killer Bug – originally called the Grayling Bug and only renamed when it was found to be just as effective as a taker of trout. Other patterns that serve at least as well include a number of shrimp patterns, heavily weighted dressings of traditional nymph patterns such as the Depth Charge Pheasant Tail nymph, and the more modern series of Polish Woven nymphs and Czech Mates.

As a rule of thumb, leaders for fishing these heavy patterns should be between twice and three times as long as the depth of the water, depending on the speed of the current. I generally make up these long leaders by using a blood knot to secure about 4 feet of 20 pound nylon to the braided loop on the fly-line; blood-knotting a further, say, 3 feet of 16 pound nylon to this; blood-knotting the front 8½ feet of a 9 foot, 4X (4 pound) knotless tapered leader to the 16 pound nylon; and finally adding an 18 inch tippet of 3 pound nylon to the point of the leader using a three-turn water knot. In this case, my leader is about 17 feet long, which will allow me to fish a pool between 6 and 9 feet deep with a moderate flow of water running through it. The overall length of the leader can be increased or decreased by using a longer or shorter 16 pound middle section.

The prospect of casting with long leaders and heavy artificials may seem a daunting one, especially to the novice. Wind knots certainly appear in the nylon much more readily than with more traditional terminal tackle. The key to success is to slow down the casting rate, and to pause for significantly longer on the back-cast than you normally would in order to make absolutely certain that the fly-line and leader are straightening fully in the air behind you before starting the forward cast.

The difficulty of detecting takes is rather less easily resolved. A grayling can take a deep-sunk artificial very gently indeed, causing the nylon on the water's surface to pause only momentarily or, often, not at all, and can spit it out again instantaneously on discovering its mistake. Of course, the top 3 or 4 feet of nylon can and should be greased to make them more visible but, even on calm water, nylon can be very difficult to see in flat, grey, autumn and winter light. While I have strong reservations about using them for summer nymphing for trout, a useful aid to take detection when grayling fishing in the autumn or winter is a strike indicator, available from tackle shops, serving very much like a coarse angler's float. If you do not have one, half an inch of white or brightly coloured wool, well greased with Mucilin and hitched to the butt length of the leader, can be almost as good.

When nymph fishing for unseen grayling, you must learn to tighten at the slightest change in the leader's behaviour, without waiting to ask whether it was caused by a fish or not. You may waste a little time striking as the artificial bumps into boulders on the bottom or snags on the odd bit of weed, but it is amazing how often you will be rewarded with a solid pull and a well-bent rod. The upstream strike, described in Chapter 7, is particularly useful when fishing for deep-feeding grayling.

So, when no fish are showing at the surface – which is likely to be for the majority of the time – you must prospect for them, moving steadily upstream, dropping weighted nymphs or shrimps into likely runs or pools. Start at the bottom end of each stretch and fish the water carefully, paying particular attention to deep holes, steep undercut banks, glides beneath overhanging bushes and the slack water above hatches and weirs and adjacent to the boils below them. And, when you catch a fish, remain at the same spot for a while, remembering that where one has been willing to take your fly, her brothers and sisters may be equally keen to follow suit.

Wet-Fly Fishing

Between deep nymph fishing and dry-fly fishing comes the wet fly, probably the most traditional and widely used method on all grayling rivers apart from the chalk streams, where nymph and dry-fly fishing still predominate.

The techniques used for wet-fly fishing for grayling are much the same as those for trout, and the arguments for and against fishing upstream or across and down are similar, too. Many grayling anglers, particularly in the north country, still fish across and down, chiefly because it enables them to cover more water than they could by casting upstream. But logic suggests that upstream fishing should be more effective, allowing flies to sink deeper and pricking fewer fish.

Whichever style is chosen, wet-fly patterns for grayling can be selected along very much the same lines as dry flies, with imitative or food-suggesting dressings such as the Greenwell's Spider and the Black Pennell and the Snipe series of spider patterns working well in low or clear water conditions. Slightly gaudier fancy flies such as the Partridge and Orange and a Red Tag fished wet may be needed as the water becomes more coloured or swollen.

Grayling can be fussy feeders on occasions, ignoring one fancy pattern but taking another apparently very similar one enthusiastically, and their preferences seem to vary from river to river and from day to day. If you are unsure about what is likely to interest them, it is worth trying a team of two or three, perhaps putting a weighted dressing on the point. And, as always, if you are unfamiliar with a particular water, it always pays to seek informed local advice.

Dry-Fly Fishing

Unlike trout, grayling tend to rise to surface flies in the coldest, most blustery and least comfortable weather, provided that the water is clear enough for them to see what is going on above them and that there is something for them to rise to. Also unlike trout, they almost invariably remain close to the river bed during a hatch, climbing steeply and tipping over almost on to their backs to take the flies, returning to the bottom as soon as they have done so. The rise is distinctive – slightly splashy, often leaving a bubble drifting away on the surface, and very, very quick. Those who have just spent six months counting to three before hooking trout often find it difficult to come to terms with the speed of response demanded by grayling.

Grayling also differ from trout in the marked preference they show for attractor flies. Where brown and rainbow trout will often ignore a dry fly that does not approximate quite accurately in size, shape and colour to the naturals upon which they are feeding, grayling can often be taken more readily on pretty, fancy patterns – especially those with a bit of red or yellow or a twist of gold or silver in their make-ups – than they can on a more precise imitation. For myself, I would be quite content to go in pursuit of grayling armed with nothing more than a few Red Tags, Treacle Parkins and Grayling Witches to supplement the dry flies I normally use for trout, and the Killer Bugs and weighted nymphs with which I search out deep-feeding fish.

One of the favours the grayling bestows is that, provided she's not pricked, she will often rise obligingly to a dry fly again and again. A grayling having risen to a fly and missed it (or been missed) a couple of times, should not persuade you to move on as you might if casting to trout. If you have not alarmed her, either by letting her feel the point of the hook or by showing yourself to her, there is every possibility that she will repeat the attempt. And if she does not, there is every likelihood that one of her companions in the shoal of which she is almost certainly a part may take up the challenge.

Those who have only ever caught grayling in the summer may be startled by the ferocity with which an autumn or winter fish can fight. Even a half- or three-quarter pounder can provide some heart-stopping moments, especially if she gets downstream of you in fast water and then uses her enormous dorsal fin as a paravane, tracking back and forth across the current – which is another argument for casting upstream. Fishing across and down confronts us with the near-inevitability of having to cope with the problems of playing a fish downstream.

As with trout, if grayling are to be released you should use barbless hooks and the fish should be freed without being removed from the water. If they are required for the table – and the grayling is an excellent table fish – they should be dispatched quickly and humanely.

Grayling fishing is a wonderful sport in its own right and provides a most welcome extension to the trout season. On many waters that hold both trout and grayling, it is possible to fish for as much as eleven months in the year. So let us salute the grayling, rather than castigate her; she is a wonderfully pretty fish and a fine adversary, and she makes a marvellous breakfast.

12   Looking Ahead

Every week, the first page of *The Shooting Times & Country Magazine* carries a quotation from King George VI: 'The wildlife of today is not ours to dispose of as we please. We have it in trust. We must account for it to those who come after.' That goes for our fishing, too.

While there is still a wealth of wonderful fishing to be had in Britain, much of it remarkably inexpensive, there can be little doubt that our sport is facing greater threats and challenges now than ever before – from degradation of the streams and rivers and of their catchment areas; from antis; from a public whose often whimsical perceptions of the natural world owe more than they should to Beatrix Potter and Walt Disney; and from politicians with scant knowledge of the countryside and a propensity for banning things they don't understand.

One of the most effective ways in which angling may defend itself against all this is by ensuring that it makes a substantial and demonstrable contribution to conservation and to the environment, and that in doing so it attracts the respect and support of non-angling conservationists and of the public at large. This need not be so uphill a battle as it may seem. It must be twenty years since Friends of the Earth first described anglers as 'the natural custodians of our watercourses'. Much more recently, in May 2001, it was heartening to hear the eminent naturalist, David Bellamy, saying much the same at the launch of a restoration project on the River Wandle.

It is not enough, though, simply to persuade such people that we have a significant role to play. We must fulfil that role proactively, taking the lead, collaborating with Wildlife and River Trusts, English

Nature, the Environment Agency and other conservation bodies, and setting the highest possible standards for the management and conservation of aquatic environments.

There is one organization in particular that is putting this concept into practice. Established in 1997, the Wild Trout Trust aims to bring together individuals, fishing clubs and syndicates, riparian owners and people involved commercially in wild trout fishing to promote conservation through education, raising the profile of the wild trout and of the issues fundamental to its welfare; to run restoration projects; and to encourage its members to be active in looking after wild trout habitats and in countering the influences that threaten them. It does all this in an extraordinarily energetic, imaginative and focused way, collaborating closely with a remarkable range of non-angling bodies. I really do not believe anyone can go trout fishing with a clear conscience nowadays unless they actively support the Trust's work. The Trust's contact details may be found at Appendix 2.

One issue that requires urgent action, and in which anglers can and must play a leading role, has to do with the very alarming decline in chalk-stream fly life in recent years. The full extent of the problem did not become apparent until 2001, when Allan Frake of the Environment Agency and Peter Hayes of the Wiltshire Fisheries Association co-published their *Report on the Millennium Chalk Streams Fly Trends Study*.

The background to the study was the realization that, while flyfishers, river keepers and riparian owners all bemoaned the 'chalk stream malaise' – the reported decline in the general condition of the Hampshire and Wessex chalk streams – no quantitative evidence was available to support or refute reports of fewer fly. The problem was compounded by the fact that the reports came largely from anglers and the authorities therefore regarded them as anecdotal and biased. It was compounded further by the Environment Agency's method of monitoring, which, based on finding but not counting nymphs, showed that all species were present and correct and there appeared, therefore, to be no cause for concern.

Carefully crafted questionnaires were sent out to 1,500 anglers, river keepers, club and syndicate secretaries and riparian owners, using the membership lists of clubs, syndicates and fishery associations. Since angling access to the southern chalk streams is generally available chiefly through such organizations, the survey's coverage was able to be particularly comprehensive.

The questionnaires asked people to go back as far as they could through memory and, where possible, written records, and to report how many times they had been on each river recently, on the abundance of fly hatches in general and, where practicable, on the abundance of particular fly species. Respondents were asked to score fly abundance using a code that ranged from 'good hatches frequently' through 'good hatches infrequently', 'sparse hatches frequently', 'sparse hatches infrequently' and 'very little fly' to 'absent'.

Three hundred and sixty-five questionnaires were returned, 109 of them by people who had worked from written records. Of the 365, 89 were keepers, owners or club officials, most of whom spend a great deal of time on river banks. The responses were analysed in groups – before 1939, in decades until 1989 and then from 1990–94, 1995–97, 1998 and 1999.

It might be supposed that people's memories would prove markedly more fallible than written records. Indeed, those working solely from memory did produce slightly better reports of fly abundance during the decades from the 1940s to the 1960s, and slightly less good ones in the more recent decades. But the differences were really quite small, written records matching recollection remarkably closely.

The results show a slight and gradual decline in general fly abundance between 1940 and 1980, a more marked decline in the 1980s and then a precipitous one in the early 1990s. The mayfly's decline was found to have been rather less dramatic than that of smaller fly species, the iron blue and the blue-winged olive being the worst affected. Overall, the scores for fly abundance fell from a benchmark 100 before the Second World War to 34 at the end of 1999.

The outcomes mirror closely the declines in birds and butterflies that have been identified by other surveys – an average population decline of 40 per cent among the twenty species included in the Government's Farmland Bird Index, a greater than 50 per cent decline in a third of butterfly species, and declines greater than 20 per cent in many other butterfly species.

While the study makes gloomy reading, it does at least demonstrate one of the roles that anglers have to play in monitoring the health of aquatic environments.

Numerous theories have been put forward about why insect abundance has declined so suddenly and dramatically. Endocrine disrupters such as Ethinyl estradiol, a synthetic oestrogen used in oral contraceptives, enter rivers through sewage systems, which do not filter them out. Increasing levels of oestrogen in watercourses have been shown significantly to alter the gender balance in fish populations, and it would be interesting to know whether they may be having the same effect on aquatic invertebrates.

Sheep dips are lethal to insects – that is their purpose. There is always a risk that they may leach into streams and rivers, and some of the newer ones have been shown to be as much as a hundred times more toxic than traditional organophosphate dips in water. Synthetic pyrethroid dips cause particular concern because of their extreme toxicity to both invertebrates and fish. The use of such dips has increased recently as the use of organophosphate pesticides, which can cause illness in humans, has been phased out.

Another possible culprit are anthelmintics, a group of chemicals used for worming livestock. Manure from the treated animals contains traces of anthelmintics. Insects lay their eggs in the fresh manure, but their newly hatched larvae are killed by the drug residues. Research into dung beetles has shown their mortality rates to be extremely high because of the efficiency with which they detect fresh manure. But it may be, also, that the anthelmintics are leaching into watercourses from the meadows and killing aquatic insects' nymphs and larvae.

More speculative is the coincidence of timing between the introduction of unleaded petrol in the mid 1980s and the sudden beginning of a very serious down-turn in fly-life abundance. Unleaded petrol is no cleaner than leaded petrol; it was simply introduced to allow the use of catalytic converters, which reduce the levels of sulphur dioxide and nitrogen oxide in exhaust gasses, but which are themselves destroyed by lead. Several of the ingredients of unleaded petrol are said to be powerful herbicides and insecticides, which gives rise to the question of whether the exhaust gasses from vehicles using unleaded petrol may be damaging insect populations either directly, in the atmosphere, or indirectly, through run-off water from roads. It is certainly the case that summer days when one spent time and effort cleaning dead insects from car windscreens are long gone.

Then there is the increase in blue-green algae, which may be toxic to the larvae of invertebrates or disruptive of their food supplies. Blue-green algal blooms usually appear in warm, still, humid weather in summer or early autumn, and their incidence appears to have been increasing as the British climate has become warmer. In recent years, blue-green algae have been responsible for the deaths of birds, fish and animals in the UK, and there is no reason to suppose that they are any less lethal to insects. They are also associated with eutrophication – the enrichment of water, usually by phosphates and nitrogen, and its consequent de-oxygenation.

More mysterious has been an apparent reduction in the adherent properties of the egg balls of at least one up-winged fly, the blue-winged olive (B-WO). For the past ten years, Dr Cyril Bennett, an entomologist specializing in freshwater invertebrates, has maintained a blue-winged olive farm in his study – simply a small, water-filled glass tank containing a number of microscope slides. Each slide has three or four roundish, greyish patches on it – its share of the farm's B-WO eggs, which Cyril collects from female spinners at the waterside. The eggs usually stick fairly quickly to the slides but it seems to have become more difficult for them to do so in recent years. If they come unstuck within the first twelve hours, it is sometimes possible to re-stick them. After twelve hours, though, the adhesive coating appears to have gone and they are no longer able to re-adhere.

Of itself, that may appear to be of little more than academic interest. But John Goddard, another eminent angling entomologist has recently seen clouds of female B-WO spinners dancing above the River Test with not a single egg ball among them. We know that, having extruded their eggs, B-WO spinners use their tails to press their egg balls to the undersides of their abdomens, where they are held in position by the stickiness of the egg mass. Could it be that the egg balls are dropping off, rather than adhering, simply because they have lost their sticki-ness? And, if so, what has caused that, and could it be that other aquatic flies have been similarly affected?

The answer to the essential question of why fly hatches have declined so dramatically over the past fifteen or twenty years may, of course, lie in one, some, all or none of these hypotheses. What they demonstrate, though, is the potential complexity of the research that may be necessary to identify the cause of the decline. But that research must be done and the damage must be reversed. Aquatic invertebrates represent an essential link in the food chain, providing food for a wide range of fish and bird species. They are 'miner's canaries', indicators of the state of a river's health. As flyfishers, we watch them more closely than most, and we have a moral responsibility to draw the attention of conservation bodies and government to any significant reduction in their numbers, and to press for appropriate action.

Although the damage done to river fisheries by fish-eating birds – cormorants, goosanders and mergansers (sawbill ducks) – is far less mysterious than the decline in fly life, the solutions seem almost as difficult to find.

All wild birds are protected under the Wildlife and Countryside Act, 1981, which prohibits their being killed or taken, or their eggs or nests being taken or destroyed, except under licence.

Cormorant numbers have increased rapidly throughout Europe in recent years. Between 1987 and 1994, the British breeding population increased at a rate of about 3 per cent per annum and the numbers of birds spending the winters on inland waters rose at between 5 and 10 per cent per annum. Thereafter, the population appears to have stabilized with an over-wintering population of between 15,000 and 16,000 birds. The sawbill population has been growing, too, with the over-wintering population currently estimated at around 9,000 birds.

Cormorants tend to congregate chiefly in lowland areas, often around stillwater fisheries, but they take significant numbers of fish from rivers, too. Sawbills generally breed in upland areas in the spring, mothers and young frequenting upland streams throughout the summer. The highest concentrations of sawbills on the lower reaches of rivers tend to occur in midwinter.

Cormorants and sawbills are opportunistic predators, eating a wide variety of fish species, including trout, grayling and salmon parr, and in significant numbers. There can be no doubt that they do substantial damage to present and future fish stocks or that the damage they do has increased in line with the increase in the numbers of resident birds.

None but the most unthinking angler would wish to see cormorants or sawbills exterminated, but there is a balance to be struck – sustainable populations of fish-eating birds need to be balanced with equally sustainable populations of fish. The chief problem in achieving this lies in the fact that while cormorants and sawbills are quite easy to count, fish are not, and it is therefore difficult to demonstrate the damage that is being done.

Again, the solution must lie in collaboration between fishery owners and managers, conservation organizations such as the Royal Society for the Protection of Birds, and the government.

If the harm done to fish stocks by fish-eating birds is difficult to prove, the damage done to sea-trout runs by salmon farming is far less so. The geographical and historic coincidences of estuarine salmon farming on the one hand and declining sea-trout stocks on the other is obvious and clearly demonstrable, as is the cause of the reduction in sea-trout numbers. As we saw in Chapter 10, sea-trout runs in rivers with estuarine salmon farming have generally been reduced to trickles by vast numbers of sea lice emanating from the salmon farms and infesting seaward-bound sea-trout smolts. It takes only about thirty sea lice to kill a sea trout smolt; fish found in lochs and rivers affected by estuarine salmon farming have been found to be infested with 200 or more. In the many places in which there is no salmon farming, numbers of sea lice have generally remained steady and there are still excellent runs of sea trout.

The difficulty appears to be that salmon farming is big business and that money talks. While privately recognizing the cause of the decline in sea trout-numbers, and despite pressure from angling and conservation interests, the governments concerned have so far proved very reluctant to acknowledge the problem publicly and take steps to resolve it.

That must surely change. What is reassuring is that, brown trout and sea trout being one and the same species, there is reasonable certainty that, in any river with a healthy brown-trout population, sea-trout runs will resume when the sea lice have been eradicated.

All these issues – the setting of high standards in fisheries management, finding and reversing the causes of the decline in fly life, balancing sustainable fish-eating bird populations with equally sustainable fish populations, and restoring lost sea-trout runs – are best dealt with by those who represent us and to whom we should therefore lend our support. The Salmon & Trout Association, the governing body for game angling in the United Kingdom, does stalwart work in addressing such matters. Contact details are at Appendix 2, as are details of the Anglers' Conservation Association, the excellent organization established specifically to prosecute those who pollute angling waters.

On a more personal level, and apart from actively supporting the bodies that promote and represent our interests, there are things that we ourselves can do to safeguard the future of our sport.

The first is to introduce others, and especially young people, to it. The Salmon & Trout Association has long recognized this and runs numerous beginners' courses around the country. But we as individuals can do our bit, too, and there is great satisfaction and pleasure to be had from seeing enthusiasm and excitement build as beginners catch their first few trout.

The second, which goes almost without saying, is that we should do whatever we can to avoid causing any harm either to the environment or to the sport of others.

Respect for the environment is neatly summed up in the countryside code: enjoy the countryside and respect its life and work; guard against all risk of fire; fasten all gates; keep dogs under close control; keep to public paths across farmland; use gates and stiles to cross fences, hedges and walls; leave livestock, crops and machinery alone; take your litter home (especially loose lengths of nylon and the like); help keep all water clean; protect wildlife, plants and trees; take special care on country roads; and make no unnecessary noise.

Respect for fellow anglers is just as simple. It has to do with obeying the fishery rules; giving other people space; not disturbing the water unnecessarily – for example, keeping well away from the river when walking downstream; and avoiding harrying fish unnecessarily,

making them warier than they naturally are and therefore more difficult to catch.

Third, we need to practise restraint. In the United States, 'limit your
catch, don't catch your limit' is a catchphrase widely used by the State
Departments of Fish and Game, which manage public angling waters.
It is equally applicable elsewhere. Far too many anglers are afflicted
with 'limititis', gauging the success of a day by whether they caught
the maximum number of fish allowed or not, and feeling they have
failed in some way when they do not do so. That is a pity because it
makes for fishing that will quite often be disappointing, and it has the
potential to make unacceptable inroads into finite trout and grayling
populations.

Finally, I am sure it helps to remember that quotation from Ed Zern,
the doyen of American fishing writers: 'Fly fishing, or any other sport
fishing, is an end in itself and not a game or competition among fishermen.'

Appendix 1

The Flyfisher's Knots

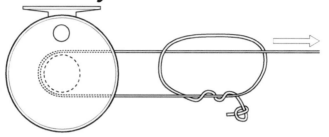

Slip knot: for securing backing line to a reel

WRONG: the leader loop will eventually cut into the braided one

RIGHT: the tension will be evenly distributed

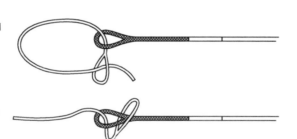

The loop-to-loop joining of a leader to a braided loop

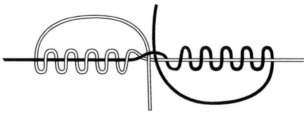

Four-turn blood knot for joining two lenghts of reasonably heavy monofilament (say, 6 lbs+) of not greatly dissimilar diameter. Moisten well before pulling tight.

Fig. 22

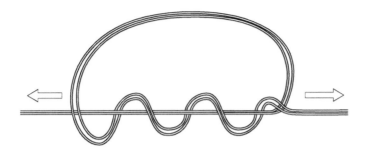

Three-turn water knot: the most reliable knot for joining two lenghts of nylon and for forming droppers. Moisten well before pulling tight.

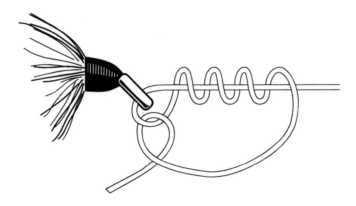

Tucked half-blood knot for tying flies to leaders.
Moisten well before pulling tight.

Fig. 23

Appendix 2

Signposts

This appendix provides contact details for a range of organizations and businesses that regulate or offer fishing, or are worthy of our support because of the work they do to secure the sport's future.

Before considering sources of fishing, we need to remember that wherever and whenever we go fishing we must have permission from the owner of the water and that, in England and Wales, anyone aged twelve years or over who fishes for salmon, trout, freshwater fish or eels must have an Environment Agency (EA) rod licence. The same goes for anyone aged eighteen or over in Northern Ireland.

England and Wales

The EA are to be applauded for the lengths they have gone to in making it easy to buy a rod licence. Until quite recently, each of the ten water authorities in England and Wales sold their own licences, which made life difficult for those who fished around the country, especially as licences were only available from a relatively small number of outlets.

Nowadays, a single licensing system covers the whole of England and Wales and licences can be bought from all post offices as well as directly from the EA's website at *www.environment-agency.gov.uk/subjects/fish*. Alternatively, you can buy your licence annually by direct debit, which saves even having to think about it. Details of local EA offices are available through the general enquiry line 0845 9333111.

Scotland

There is no national rod-licensing system in Scotland where anglers need only a 'written right or permission' from the landowner. Such permission is essential throughout Scotland if you are fishing for salmon or sea trout. Where brown trout and grayling are concerned, the situation is a little more complicated and depends on whether the water is covered by a protection order. A list of the areas under protection orders can be found at the Scottish Federation for Coarse Angling's website at *www.sfca.co.uk* under 'policy'. No fishing of any sort is allowed in Scotland on Sundays.

Northern Ireland

Rod licences are issued by the Fisheries Conservancy Board for Northern Ireland (1 Mahon Road, Portadown, Co. Armagh, BT62 3EE), which covers all fisheries apart from those controlled by the Foyle Fisheries Commission (8 Victoria Road, Londonderry, BT47 2AB). Over the age of eighteen, a rod licence is required if fishing for salmon or sea trout anywhere in Northern Ireland and for game fishing generally in the Foyle area.

Finding Fishing

There are several excellent sources of information about publicly accessible fishing, the longest established being *Where to Fish*, which is published biennially by the Thomas Harmsworth Publishing Company. Containing a wealth of information about fishing through-out the British Isles and abroad, its content is also available on the Internet at *www.where-to-fish.com*.

Other useful websites include:

www.fishandfly.co.uk
www.fishing-in-wales.com
www.fishing-scotland.net
www.fishireland.com

For those who may be interested in visiting the places where most of the photographs for this book were taken, all of which I can recom-mend, they are:

The Arundell Arms, Lifton, Devon, PL16 0AA (tel: 01566 784666; fax: 01566 784494; *www.arundellarms.com*) is extremely comfortable and has twenty miles of excellent brown-trout and sea-trout fishing on its own water on the Tamar and five of its tributaries.

The Duchy of Cornwall offers twenty-seven miles of first-class brown-trout, sea-trout and salmon fishing on the Upper Dart at extremely reasonable cost. Tickets are available from several outlets, all of them listed on the Get Hooked website at *www.gethooked.co.uk* (use 'Fishfinder' > search for River Dart > Duchy of Cornwall).

The Half Moon Inn, Sheepwash, Beaworthy, N. Devon, EX21 15NE (tel: 01409 231376) is comfortable and homely, and has ten miles of excellent brown-trout and sea-trout fishing on the River Torridge.

Wessex Fly Fishing, Lawrence's Farm, Tolpuddle, Dorchester, Dorset, DT2 7HF (tel: 01305 848460; *www.goflyfishing.co.uk*) offers comfortable holiday cottages and bed and breakfast, and has several miles of excellent brown-trout fishing on the rivers Frome and Piddle and their tributaries and carriers.

Books

For those who would delve deeper into particular aspects of river fly-fishing, antiquarian and out-of-print angling books may be obtained from:

Coch-y-Bonddu Books, Papyrus, Pentrehedyn Street, Machynlleth, Powys, SY20 8DJ (tel: 01654 702837; fax: 01654 702857)

The Barn Book Supply, 88 Crane Street, Salisbury, Wiltshire, SP1 2QD (tel: 01722 327767; *info@johnandjudithhead.co.uk*; *www.hollom.demon.co.uk*)

or from website: *www.abebooks.com*

And Deserving of Our Support

The Anglers' Conservation Association, Eastwood House, 6 Rainbow Street, Leominster, Herefordshire, HR6 8DQ (*www.a-c-a.org/default.asp*) is the body that exists to prosecute those who pollute angling waters. It has lost only two cases since it was founded in 1949.

The Grayling Society exists to promote and conserve the grayling as a true game fish. As it is run entirely, and very efficiently, by volunteers, and because officers change from time to time, contact details for the Membership Secretary should be obtained from the Society's handsome and very comprehensive website at *www.graylingsociety.org.*

The governing body for game angling in the UK is The Salmon & Trout Association, Fishmongers' Hall, London Bridge, London EC4R 9EL; (tel: 020 7283 5838; fax: 020 7626 5137, *www.salmon-trout.org*). Its Scottish arm is The Salmon & Trout Association (Scotland), The National Game Angling Centre, The Pier, Loch Leven, Kinross KY13 8UF; (tel: 01577 861116; fax: 01577 864769).

The Wild Trout Trust brings together individuals, fishing clubs and syndicates, riparian owners and people involved commercially in wild trout fishing to raise the profile of the wild trout and of the issues fundamental to its welfare; to run restoration projects; and to encourage its members to be active in looking after wild trout habitats and in countering the influences that threaten them. It can be contacted at The Wild Trout Trust, PO Box 120, Waterlooville, PO8 0WZ (tel: 023 9257 0985) or through its exceptional website at *www.wildtrout.org.*

Bibliography

Barker, Thomas, *Barker's Delight or The Art of Angling*, 2nd edn (1659)

Broughton, Ronald, *The Complete Book of the Grayling*, 2nd edn (Robert Hale, 2000)

Buller, F., 'The Earliest Fishing Reel – A New Perspective' (*Flyfishers Journal*, Vol. 85, No. 305, Summer 1998), pp.9–15

Buller, F., 'The Macedonian Fly' (*Flyfishers Journal*, Vol. 85, No. 303, Summer 1997), pp.17–21.

Buller F. and Falkus H., *Falkus & Buller's Freshwater Fishing* (Macdonald and Jane's, 1975)

Clarke, Brian, and Goddard, John, *The Trout and the Fly* (Ernest Benn Limited, 1980)

Frake, A. and Hayes, P., *Report on the Millennium Chalk Streams Fly Trends Study* (Environment Agency, 2001)

Frost W.E. and Brown, M.E., *The Trout* (Collins, 1967)

Goddard, John, *Trout Flies of Britain and Europe* (Robert Hale, 2001)

Goddard, John, *Trout Fly Recognition*, 2nd edn (A & C Black, 1991)

Goddard, John, *Waterside Guide* (Unwin Hyman, 1988)

Goddard, John, *John Goddard's Trout Fishing Techniques*, (A & C Black, 1996)

Grubic, G. and Herd A., 'Astraeus: The First Fly-Fishing River' (*The American Fly Fisher*, Vol. 27, No. 4, Fall 2001), pp. 16–22

Halford, F.M., *Floating Flies and How to Dress Them* (1886)

Halford, F.M., *Dry-Fly Fishing in Theory and Practice* (1889)

Halford, F.M., *An Angler's Autobiography* (1903)

Halford, F.M., *Modern Development of the Dry Fly* (1910)

Halford, F.M., *The Dry Fly Man's Handbook* (1913)

Harris, Graeme, and Morgan, Moc, *Successful Sea Trout Angling* (Blandford Press, 1989)

Hayter, Tony, *F.M. Halford and the Dry-Fly Revolution* (Robert Hale, 2002)

Herd, Andrew, *The Fly* (The Medlar Press, 2001)

Hoffmann, Richard C., *Fishers' Craft and Lettered Art* (University of Toronto Press, 1997)

Lapsley, Peter, *Fishing for Falklands Sea Trout* (Falkland Islands Tourist Board, 2000)

McDonald, John, *The Origins of Angling* (Lyons & Burford, 1957)

Mackie, Gordon, *Fly Leaves and Waterside Sketches* (Robert Hale, 1998)

Marinaro, Vincent, *In the Ring of the Rise* (Robert Hale, 1999)

O'Reilly, Peter, *Rivers of Ireland* (Merlin Unwin Books, 1991)

Patterson, Neil, *Chalkstream Chronicle* (Merlin Unwin Books, 1995)

Pritt, T.E., *North Country Flies* (1886)

Pulman, G.P.R., *The Vade Mecum of Fly Fishing for Trout* (1841)

Radcliffe, William, *Fishing from Earliest Times* (Murray, 1921)

Ronalds, Alfred, *The Fly-Fisher's Entomology* (Longmans Green, 1836)

Sandison, Bruce, *Game Fishing in Scotland* (Mainstream Publishing, 1988)

Schullery, Paul, *Royal Coachman* (Simon & Schuster, New York, 1999)

Skues, G.E.M., *Itchen Memories* (Robert Hale, 1999)

Skues, G.E.M., *Minor Tactics of the Chalk Stream*, (A & C Black, 1910)

Skues, G.E.M., *The Way of a Trout with a Fly* (A & C Black, 1921)

Skues, G.E.M., *Side-lines, Side-lights & Reflections* (Seeley Service, 1932)

Skues, G.E.M., *Nymph Fishing for Chalk Stream Trout* (A & C Black, 1939)

Stewart, W.C., *The Practical Angler* (1857)

Stolz, J. and Schnell, J., (eds) *Trout* (Stackpole Books, Harrisburg P.A., 1991)

Unattributed, *Where to Fish 2002–2003*, 88th edn (Thomas Harmsworth Publishing Company, 2002)

Vines, Sidney, *The English Chalk Streams* (B.T. Batsford Limited, 1992)

Viscount Grey of Falloden, *Fly Fishing*, 2nd edn (J.M. Dent and Sons, 1930)

Voss Bark, A., (ed), *West Country Fly Fishing* (Robert Hale, 1998)

Waller Hills, John, *A Summer on the Test*, 3rd edn (Hodder and Stoughton, 1941)

Walton, Izaak and Cotton, Charles, *The Compleat Angler*, Fifth Edition (1676) (Bracken Books, 1985)

Wilson, Dermot, *Fishing the Dry Fly* (A & C Black, 1970)

Index

Note: entries bracketed in bold italic – [27] or [28] – indicate photographs of flies in the colour plates